Hope and the

Future of Man

Hope and the Future of Man

EWERT H. COUSINS
Editor

FORTRESS PRESS
Philadelphia

Library of Congress Catalog Card Number 72-75647

ISBN 0-8006-0540-3

3231D 72   Printed in U.S.A.   1-540

Table of Contents

Introduction

EWERT H. COUSINS

Within the last decade we have witnessed the emergence of a new awareness of the future. Rapid change and the expanding population have forced on us long-range planning. The field of futurology has been born, and the future planner has taken his place in our society. Developments in medicine have opened a new biological future for man, and technology has made outer space a dimension of that future. Throughout the world, revolutionary movements are spurred by hope of economic and political liberation. In the midst of these new possibilities, man's future has never been more radically threatened. Nuclear weapons and the ecological crisis raise the basic question: Does man have a future? What kind of hope can he have for the future?

In theology, the future has come into new prominence. Instead of being viewed as outside time, God is seen as intimately involved in the temporal process, and Christ is viewed as the energy source of evolution. Eschatology has been singled out as the distinctive element in the Christian vision, and hope the central Christian virtue.

It was in this context that the Conference on Hope and the Future of Man was conceived, planned, and executed. Held in New York City on October 8-10, 1971, the conference was sponsored by the American Teilhard de Chardin Association, the Cardinal

Bea Institute of Woodstock College, Goethe House New York (a branch of Goethe Institute Munich), Trinity Institute, and Union Theological Seminary, with the cooperation of the Riverside Church.

The conference was the first in a two-stage project. This first stage drew together leading thinkers of three theological currents seriously concerned with the future: theologians of hope from Germany, American process theologians, and Teilhardians. These three groups met to explore their understanding of the future; to present, clarify, and refine their respective models of the future. Their point of departure was the question: What do you mean by the future?

The present volume contains the six public lectures of the conference along with seven responses, and concludes with an afterword by Daniel Day Williams. The second stage of the project is planned to take place within a year or two of the first. This will bring the same groups of theologians together with future planners: technologists, scientists, sociologists, and political scientists who are actively engaged in planning the future.

In the last few years, a number of conferences have been held on the future and on hope. This conference was unique in that it drew together for the first time process theologians, Teilhardians, and theologians of hope. Although they have been in contact in various ways, they had never met for a mutual exchange over their understanding of the future. The conference, then, reflected a major crystallization of the consciousness of the future in the theological community at the present time. These three groups do more than mirror a general trend in our culture; they provide rich resources for man to understand himself in a world in which the future is becoming more and more challenging. They provide models for the future and search out the basis for man's hope in the future. Sensitive to the problems of our time, these three groups have attempted to bring to light the values which will energize man in building his future. The conference attempted to identify these resources, to clarify them by critical dialogue, and to make them available in the larger community.

Process theology is derived from the metaphysics of Alfred North Whitehead, whose thought reflects the revolution in science brought about by Einstein's theory of relativity. Whitehead stressed the radically temporal nature of reality, spoke of events rather than substances, and saw process as fundamental to the world and God. Process theologians have found Whitehead's thought more effective than classical metaphysics to articulate the biblical message—which stresses God's involvement in the temporal process. Pierre Teilhard de Chardin reflects the revolution in biology effected by Darwin's theory of evolution. A paleontologist who spent many years on field trips in the Orient, Teilhard developed a worldview that made evolution central. From the atom to man, the entire universe is evolving toward increased consciousness. By reading the past, we can discern the direction of evolution and obtain guidelines for creative action toward building the future. Teilhard interpreted the Christian message in terms of evolution and saw Christ as the Omega or energizing focal point of the process. The theology of hope, which developed in Germany, reflects biblical research into eschatology and certain strands of German philosophy, especially Hegel, Marx, and Bloch. At the core of the biblical message is God's promise of future fulfillment and the hope it engenders. God's promise spurs man to liberate himself from the limits of his present situation. The future, as God's power, can burst in upon the present bringing something radically new, unexpected, beyond man's dreams.

The conference began with three position papers on the meaning of the future. John Cobb spoke from a process point of view, Philip Hefner from a Teilhardian perspective, and Carl Braaten from the hope or eschatological point of view. These papers are printed as the first three selections in the present volume. Their purpose was to set the stage for the discussion that was to follow. The three visitors from Germany—Jürgen Moltmann, Wolfhart Pannenberg, and Johannes Metz—gave responses to these presentations, and the American speakers responded to them. On each evening of the conference, a public lecture was given by one of the German theologians, and responses were made by two American theologians:

one representing a Teilhardian and the other a process point of view. These three lectures and the six responses are published in the present volume.

The public lectures, held in the nave of the Riverside Church, attracted large crowds ranging from 800 to 1500. Some 400 attended a special session for students held at Union Seminary, at which the conference speakers answered questions. Since there was no formal registration, the audience varied over the three days, with an estimated total of over 2500 people in attendance. Although the majority of the audience was from the New York area, many traveled from distant points in the United States and Canada.

In addition to the public sessions, three working sessions were held: two at Woodstock College and one at Union Seminary. The purpose of these sessions was to discuss in greater detail and technical precision the issues that emerged in the public sessions. Present at these sessions were the twelve conference speakers and some twenty other invited specialists, among whom were Charles Hartshorne, Theodosius Dobzhansky, Bernard Meland, and N. M. Wildiers. Schubert Ogden served as seminar leader for the first two sessions, and Daniel Day Williams for the third. Since discussion at the working sessions moved over a wide range and involved many speakers, it did not seem practical to include this material in the present volume. We can merely indicate the chief issues and the direction the discussion took.

The issue discussed at the first working session had been raised by Moltmann the previous afternoon. In his response to the initial talks, which is included in this volume, he proposed a radical criticism of the conference and challenged the speculative approach of the Whiteheadians and Teilhardians. The conference had begun by exploring the question: What do you mean by the future? This would not be Moltmann's first question. Rather he would ask: *Whose* future? *Whose* hopes? The future and hope are tied to specific interest groups: to the black community, the third world. Pure theory about the future is abstract. A future that can be related to God must begin with overcoming the oppression of the present. In his response, Pannenberg defended theoretical discussion against Moltmann's critique. If we dismiss theoretical discussion, Pannenberg said, we dismiss one of the most powerful means of overcoming differences between people, even between the oppressed and the oppressor. Metz expressed his sympathy for social and political liberation but indicated his endorsement also of theoretical reflection. This tension between speculation and liberation was taken up in the first working session under the question: What is theology? It was understood that this question, on the nature of theology, was intended to probe the issue raised by Moltmann. The discussion ranged widely among the specialists and explored the issue from many points of view. However no striking resolution was reached; and the tension between speculative thought, on the one hand, and social and political liberation, on the other, persisted as an underlying issue throughout the conference.

The second working session was devoted to more technical questions concerning alternate ways of understanding the future, particularly the ultimate future. A major portion of the time was taken by Pannenberg, responding to questions that had arisen out of his public lecture, especially from Williams' response. Pannenberg first commented on his understanding of judgment and the ultimate destiny of man. Then defending himself against Williams' charge of Neo-Platonism, he maintained that all would not be absorbed into the One, but that a plurality of essences would remain. Finally, he addressed himself to the question of whether there will be a final event. The discussion ranged over these and similar points. Clarification was achieved in a number of areas, and many thought that this was the most profitable working session.

In the third working session, Moltmann spent some time responding to questions raised the previous evening at his public lecture. He took up Ogden's remarks on the difference between the desired future and a desirable future and the question of what is really possible. According to Moltmann, an ethic of hope would change the conditions of the possible so that what seems impossible becomes possible. Moltmann explored the relation between the oppressed creation and liberated creation. Out of this emerged a discussion of man's relation to nature. The discussion eventually moved into the question of the second phase of the project: the encounter with future planners. The keynote was provided by Richard Givens, Regional Director of the Federal Trade Commission, who is actively engaged in drawing together technologists, scientists, and economists for long-range problem solving and planning. There was no consensus reached on a specific shape and direction for the second phase of the project, but a number of models and issues were explored.

If it is difficult to convey the dynamism of these working sessions, it is impossible to recapture the many private discussions—over lunch, on walks along Riverside Drive, or at Trinity Institute, where the speakers resided. For many, these were among the richest moments of the conference. The most the present book can hope to do is to provide the reader with the formal presentations. It is hoped that these will suggest something of the complexity of the human event of the conference at the same time they convey the urgency of the issues over man's future and his hopes.

What Is the Future?

A Process Perspective

JOHN B. COBB, JR.

What is the future?

At one level there is simply no answer to this question. If one really does not know what the word future means, there is no way of explaining it to him. It is as primitive as the word yellow, whose meaning cannot be explained to one who has never seen colors. But whereas there are those who have been blind from birth and have therefore had no visual experience, we cannot conceive of one who has had no experience of time. Hence the problem is simply to point out what we mean by the future so that the questioner can identify his own experience of future within the horizon of time. That of course proves difficult, or, if we take "pointing" literally, impossible. We can only use other words, like "the not-yet" or "the will-be" to suggest or indicate what we mean. But they do not describe or define.

There has been one attempt in process philosophy to define future in a more rigorous sense. Hartshorne has proposed that the future is the indeterminate. This distinguishes it from the past that is the determinate and the present that is the becoming of determinateness or the process of determination. These are important and clarifying suggestions, and most of us here, at least, could agree that the future is indeed the indeterminate. However, if Hartshorne is saying that indeterminateness is a more primitive notion, and that "future" is identical with it in connotation as well as in denotation, I do not agree, and I think Whitehead would not have agreed. If someone argues that the future is really determinate and that its apparent indetermination is only a function of our ignorance, I disagree, but I do not regard him as uttering gibberish. The fundamental notions of future and indeterminateness are distinguishable. That the range of their reference is identical is something to be discovered and asserted. Their identity is synthetic and not analytic.

In this sense, therefore, there is no answer to the question what the future is. Past, present, and future are primitive and indefinable terms whose success in communication depends on common elements in the temporal experience of all men. We must assume that at this primal level we all mean much the same thing by future.

However, there are great differences in the way we think *about* the future and about its relation to past and present. As I have already mentioned, some think of present and future as the outworking of the past, as, therefore, already in principle fully determinate, whereas all of us here reject that view and see the future as indeterminate or open.

Other questions about the future are more obscure and difficult. Some who agree about its openness see the future as a receptacle or container already there and awaiting the filling of events. Some see only events and allow no reality to the futurity of the space-time continuum even as potentiality.

Relativity physics has created other confusions in our understanding of the future. Whereas we generally think of the line between past and future as absolute, we are now told that some events are past or future only relative to the inertial system from which the calculation is made.

Questions like these are of great importance for metaphysics, and they have more bearing upon theological discussion of the future than is usually recognized. Whitehead treated them with some thoroughness and integrated his treatment into his total conception of the future. His analysis would contribute something to our work, but it is not physical and metaphysical issues of this sort that are in view in our question. As theologians we are interested rather in questions of value and meaning. Has the future any importance for us now as human beings? If so, what meaning does it have and how is this meaning brought to bear in the present?

Eschatology or future-orientation is so fundamental to the Judeo-Christian tradition that we may assume it will play some role in almost all theology. In most of the Christian past, the decisive future has been individual judgment at death or at the final resurrection of the dead in the last days. In reaction to this view, much twentieth-century theology has turned attention from the remote future to the immediate future. Each moment is the future in which there is decisive judgment. The present ceases to be means to some distant end and becomes its own end. I will call this view existentialist.

As I understand the conception of this conference, it is a meeting of those who are dissatisifed with the existentialist interpretation of the Christian future but do not want to return to traditional other-worldly conceptions. This dissatisfaction, however, is least characteristic of Whiteheadians. For us, the Bultmannian account of Christian eschatology as openness to the immediate future is *almost* satisfactory. However, it is not, as it stands, acceptable. A modification is required; and like so many modifications that first seem moderate, this one opens the way to a range of questioning that can carry the Whiteheadian theologian *almost*, but not quite, to the conclusions of Teilhardians and theologians of hope. The main purpose of this paper will be to describe the mediating position of process theology in the tension of present and future and to appraise its relative success in dealing with the fundamental problem of historical meaning with which we are all concerned.

Whitehead shares with existentialism a focus on the present moment as the locus of decision. He agrees with the existentialist analysis that the decision moves between the two alternatives of repetition of the past and response to the new possibility that is from God. Whereas the existentialists tend to portray these alternatives as wholly exclusive of each other, so that the decision is described as either/or, Whitehead presents them as polar. The past is not merely temptation or burden, it is also potentiality. To decide for the new possibility given by God is to actualize this potentiality in a new way appropriate to the new situation. The optimal fulfillment of the new possibility is at the same time the optimum actualization of the potentiality brought to the present from the past. Where the new possibility is rejected in favor of conformity to the past, the past to which one conforms is a poor abstraction from the total past.

These differences between Whitehead's understanding of the decision before the futurity of God and that of Bultmann are important. But they focus on the relation of present to past rather than to future. In respect to the latter relation, Whitehead's doctrine of decision in the context of the aim at novel realization derived from God is remarkably similar to Bultmann's call to openness to God's future. Whitehead agrees with Bultmann that if meaning is to be found anywhere, it must be found immediately in each moment.

Whitehead does not apply the word "future" to the new possibility that is given as the ideal aim for each momentary self-act-ualization. The microscopic process of becoming in each moment is so different from the relation of successive moments to each other that temporal terms, derived from the latter, should not be applied to the former. But this is a primarily terminological question. What Bultmann means by "future" is not the ordinary sense of "future" either. Hence what first needs to be stressed is the remarkable agreement with Bultmann's existentialist analysis on the substantive point that is before us.

However, there *is* a difference on this substantive point. Bultmann is so concerned with focusing attention on the immediate future that he has little or nothing to say about the importance of the ordinary temporal future. Where he speaks of it at all, he contrasts it with the eschatological immediate futurity of God.

Whitehead, on the other hand, adopts here also a polar view of both/and over against the existential either/or. Both the immediate future *and* the future beyond itself are important to every moment. The decision that is made is, of course, only *about* the immediate realization. But it is made not only with a view to the intrinsic meaning of that realization but also with a view to how that realization will affect temporally future moments. The awareness that its realization can be a positive contribution to the temporal future is itself a part of the value realized in the moment. Thus contribution to the temporal future and present enjoyment are not to be opposed. In general, the more contribution to the future an occasion anticipates, the greater will be the meaning it experiences in its immediacy. If one concentrates only on immediate attainment without regard to its consequences, that immediate attainment is impoverished. That is to say, there is little value or interest in life when it is devoid of the sense that what is now going on has value beyond itself. In sum, Whitehead's view is that the only locus of value is the present moment, but that the richness of that value depends on anticipation of its value to others.

This is the apparently slight modification of Bultmann's existential eschatology that opens up for the process theologian the whole range of questions that concern Teilhardians and theologians of hope. If meaning in the present depends on anticipation of the temporal future, then what kind of a future do we anticipate? No question can be of more urgency for mankind than this.

Before speculating about the more remote reaches of the future, however, Whitehead calls our attention to the fact that his fundamental point is satisfied even when we limit ourselves to a quite proximate future. There would be little meaning or value to the moment in which I typed the first letter of one of these words unless in that moment I anticipated that what occurred in that moment would have consequences in successive moments as I completed that word. Much of the meaning given to each moment by anticipation of its future is of this proximate future. Whitehead thinks that in dealing with many questions about present and future we are misled by our tendency to think of the remote, rather than the imminent, future.

However, Whitehead is interested in the most comprehensive horizon as well as this very narrow one. It is not only the case that typing one letter is empty of significance when the rest of the word is not anticipated. It is also the case that typing the word has only a little meaning apart from the sentence, the sentence, apart from the paragraph, the paragraph, apart from the paper as a whole, and the paper as a whole apart from the conference for which it is intended. Even here the dependence on a wider future does not cease. There is an immediate value that we enjoy as participants in this conference. Meeting old friends and making new ones, exposure to new ideas and the expansion of horizons, intense thinking and stimulating debate, all have intrinsic value. But if we did not anticipate that what was taking place here could have beneficial consequences for us individually and perhaps even for the future development of theology, much of the enjoyment of the conference would be lost. Indeed, without such anticipation the conference would not have taken place. Furthermore, in speaking of the future development of theology we have not come to the end. Theology may have some intrinsic value, but it exists to serve the church and mankind in general. Without some dim anticipation of possible indirect benefits to humanity, it is not likely that I would find much meaning in typing a single letter. Hence Whitehead's analysis of the role of anticipation in each moment connects the meaning of the moment to the destiny of mankind.

What then is man's destiny? To ensure the meaning of the moment it seems that that destiny must be hopeful. The chain of events each of which derives its meaning from anticipation of its successors must come to rest in some end whose meaning and value does not depend on any further future. That is, there must be some fulfillment, or the whole chain falls into infinite and vicious regress. This reflection leads toward the eschatologies represented by some of you.

But Whitehead did not share that vision. For him, the course of events has neither beginning nor end. Human history, of course, does have a beginning and will have an end, but the end will be simply extinction. Even if man should evolve into something quite superior, that superior being will, in time, become extinct. For, our present purposes it does not matter much whether extinction will be within the decade or millions of years hence. The point is only that Whitehead sets our concern for meaning in the context of an infinitely extended process.

Whitehead took this infinity of process quite seriously. It did not mean for him that the physical world as we know it will endure forever. The fundamental characteristics of our universe, such as the electromagnetic field, had, he believed, a beginning in time and will have an end. What he called our cosmic epoch is but one expression of the infinite process. It evolved out of something else and will evolve into something else. The cosmic epoch from which it evolved may have had more or less intrinsic value than this one; and the same is all that can be said for future cosmic epochs. There is no assurance of progress at this most inclusive level.

Also on the scale of history, to which our imaginations are more attuned, process does not guarantee progress. Cultural epochs succeed each other, thereby realizing new and different values. Novelty is necessary if zest is to be regained after one culture has exhausted its fundamental possibilities. But whether the artistic achievements, for example, of the later epoch are greater or less than those of the earlier is an open question.

This is not a cyclic view. Whitehead stresses real novelty and radical change. Also, progress is possible. Over hundreds of millions of years and culminating in man, despite temporary reversals, there was fundamental progress on this planet in the realization of greater values. Within human history, too, threads of progress can be discerned. God's activity in the world makes for progress, as well as mere change. But there is no guarantee of progress in the short run, and in the long run it is inevitable that life on this planet will become extinct.

So far as I can tell, this vision is congenial with the best scientific knowledge and is quite plausible. There is perhaps little evidence that our electromagnetic epoch is evolving into something else, but there is certainly none against it. In general, the everlastingness of the world is more plausible to the scientifically informed mind than any idea of creation out of nothing or an end to all process.

Whitehead's view of history is fully compatible with finding penultimate meaning and hope within it. Consciously, we can live quite well most of the time with this kind of hope. But Whitehead was not satisfied with it. If this endless procession of ever new events is all there is, even if some contain richer value than others, man must see it finally as a mere "bagatelle of transient experience." The supreme importance of religion is that it gives a vision of something beyond this passing flux. Hence for Whitehead the impossibility of locating fulfillment or consummation at the temporal end of the process focused religious concern on the dimension of reality that has permanence. That is, of course, God.

To introduce God could be to solve the question of meaning for man at the expense of the meaning of history. Many Indian sages have agreed that the endless course of events is a bagatelle of experience and have turned from it to Brahman. Some Western mystics have also rejected historical meaning for mystical meaning. Orthodox Christianity has refused to sanction this rejection of history, but aspects of its official doctrine of God nevertheless have led in this direction. The understanding of God as absolute, impassible, and immutable has been hard to reconcile with the doctrine that he cares what happens in human affairs. The tension has been such that to a large extent the modern affirmation of history has involved the rejection of the Christian God.

Whitehead was deeply aware of this tension between the traditional Western picture of God and human meaning in history. He was convinced that here too a polarity was needed where all too often there had been an either/or. For Whitehead, concern for God cannot replace concern for the world. Just as the quest for meaning in the world without reference to God leads finally to a loss of meaning in the world, so a concern for God apart from a concern for the world would be faithless to God. The more we are concerned for God, the more we are concerned for the world.

This view of the polar relation of God and the world is not introduced in an *ad hoc* way into his philosophy. On the contrary it is philosophically required and richly explicated. God is not an exception to the metaphysical categories. He differs radically from all other entities especially in his universality and everlastingness, but the principle of interdependence that relates all entities applies also to him. He gives himself to the world, but the world also gives itself to him. He acts in and on every entity in the world. In turn, every entity in the world reacts upon him. Although in some respects he is absolute, in others he is absolutely relative or related. Although in some respects he is immutable, in others he shares in the processive character of all things. Far from being impassible, he is perfectly sensitive and responsive to all that happens, sharing with the world in both joy and suffering.

Whitehead works out this doctrine in terms of two natures of God which he calls primordial and consequent. The primordial nature is the organ of novelty, the ground of teleology, and the principle of concretion or determinateness in the world. The consequent nature is God as perfectly sympathetic recipient of all the values realized in the world. The primordial nature is eternal. The consequent nature is everlastingly growing. Because of the consequent nature, all process in the universe is *ultimately* progress. The value of the present is woven upon the values of the past, and together they are transformed into a new unity in God. To serve God is to give him the most value that we can. This value can be realized only in history. There can, in principle, be no tension between serving God and serving the neighbor. To serve the neighbor is to serve God, and to serve God is to serve the neighbor.

For Whitehead this vision that the penultimate value and meaning of history becomes ultimate in God saves history from being a bagatelle of experience and grounds finally the meaning of historical existence. Each moment of experience receives, as we saw, much of its internal value from its anticipation of its contribution to the future beyond itself. Insofar as it recognizes that this future contains, quite literally, God's future, its meaning has the requisite ultimacy.

To this point I have tried, in my own language and style, to be sure, to be faithful to Whitehead's view of the future and its importance in giving meaning to the present. Since encountering his thought through Hartshorne over twenty years ago I have been attracted to him and fascinated by him. Progressively my own vision of reality has been assimilated to his, at least to those aspects of his which I have understood. This process has been exceedingly enriching. If I have made any contribution to theology, it has been the result of this enrichment.

Nevertheless, neither I nor any process theologian is simply a Whiteheadian. Different aspects of Whitehead's thought have grasped us, and we have shaped them and been shaped by them in different ways. As a result, our divergences from each other are almost as important as our unity.

Whitehead's doctrine of the divine future as that which grounds meaning in the present has been central to his influence on many process theologians. Hence, at this point my exposition of Whitehead is also a generally reliable indication of the positions of his theological followers. However, I myself am interested in further, and somewhat different, reflections about the possible future. There is no time here to develop these with any clarity or fullness, but so that you may see how *one* process theologian thinks about "hope and the future of man" I will sketch my eschatological speculations.

We need a more vivid vision of the possibilities of historical existence. Such a vision can and should include political and economic elements, but ultimately the locus of reality and value is in individual entities. Unless we can envision a human existence free from the alienation, emptiness, and mutual suspicion that so deeply characterize our own, a crucial dimension of hope is undercut.

Whitehead's ontology offers a conceptuality for such a vision. The individual entities of which society is necessarily composed are not persons but units of experience. Thus far, the greatest achievement of mankind has been the ordering of these experiences successively and the unifying of these chains of experiences into personal individuals. But for this achievement we have paid the price of isolation from each other, from nature, and from our own bodies.

We need now to envision a post-personal future. In such a world there will be a rich interpenetration of each in the other to the intensification and harmonization of the experience of all. This will constitute a new kind of community transcending both collectivities and voluntary associations of autonomous persons.

The duality of nature and history will be overcome not only in concept but also in actuality. The experiences of which the human community is composed will internally incorporate the contributions of the natural environment. Man will know himself as part of nature and nature as part of himself, not to his diminishment but to his enrichment.

Spirit and flesh will be reconciled. The unrepressed body will be acknowledged as partner, and its rightful desires will be fulfilled. In this community the ancient struggle to conquer flesh for the sake of spirit will give way to the fulfillment of spirit through the flesh.

To dream of such a community may be utopian, but it is not yet eschatological. I intend to be describing a mode of existence compatible with life in this environment, in these bodies, and with sinful and suffering human beings. It would not mean the end of sickness, death, ignorance, stupidity, conflict, and disappointment. At best such communities would be limited in membership and often threatening to each other. Their achievement would provide a situation in which problems of peace, order, and justice could be more hopefully treated, but these problems would remain.

However, the realization of such a community would make more intelligible and plausible a truly eschatological vision. Such a vision would be of a mode of being requiring unforeseeable and unimaginable changes. Probably it could not be realized in corporeal existence. Perhaps it is but an idle fancy.

Our past eschatological visions have sometimes projected existing individualized and even physical conditions into a future, or an other, world. In reaction to these, others have envisioned the total absorption of all into the One. Neither vision has exercised

much attraction in modern times. Instead, men have tried to reconcile themselves to an eschatology of decay into an empty and
meaningless nothingness.

One reason for the decline of traditional Christian eschatology is
the widespread incredulity that personal selves can survive the
death of their organic base or be reconstituted on some other basis.
I have argued elsewhere that survival or reconstitution is possible.
But another objection is of a different order. Is there not something
questionable about the desire to project this private, isolated
sequence of experiences into the indefinite or even infinite future?
Is it not a selfish hope reflecting the self-preoccupation that is our
sin rather than the love that is our salvation? Must such a self not
carry with it eternally the essential problems and pains of its isolation? Would not the endless succession of experiences of this sort be
an ultimate horror rather than fulfillment?

Such questions can be answered with varying degrees of success, but the answers lack conviction and the questions keep recur-
ring. It seems that our sensibility has outgrown the individualistic
tendencies of the traditional Christian hope. Does that mean that a
new Christian existence must learn to live with an eschatology of
annihilation? I doubt that Christian existence can long survive with
that vision of reality. Hence I continue to seek a vision of eschatological fulfillment.

If we can dream of partly transcending our isolated individuality
even in this life, then our eschatological vision might share that
transcendence and go beyond it. The community for which we
hope overcomes isolation without annihilating selfhood. Perhaps we
can project a more radical overcoming of separateness which is yet
neither absorption nor annihilation but the emergence of a new
selfhood.

Whitehead affirms as a metaphysical ultimate that all process
consists in the many becoming one and being increased by one.
The many perish that the one may be born. Each one is part of a
new many which in their turn perish for the sake of the new one.
Within this process of sheer multiplicity there emerge threads of

special continuity that establish particular patterns of order. These make possible richer kinds of entities culminating finally in human experience. Here, too, the metaphysical vision applies. Each human experience is part of the many that perish so that new ones may be born.

Human experiences, as we have known them thus far, tend to constitute serial successions with peculiarly intimate connectedness. The richest values and meanings we know are the cumulative achievements of these serially ordered moments of experience. There is something unacceptable about the sheer ending of the series, and this rejection grounds the hope for everlasting life.

I am proposing a vision of a community in which the decisiveness, or at least the exclusiveness of this serial order would decline. The general metaphysical situation would then be more evidently exemplified at the level of human experiences. The many experiences of the several members of the community would perish and become one new experience in each member of the community. That is, each new experience would inherit from the past experience of all. They would constitute a new many which would in turn pass into the plurality of new units of future experience. But all of this would be very partial, limited by the peculiar connection of each experience to an incurably separate and individual body, the very narrow limits of such open communication, and the few persons with whom it can be practised.

Now let us give our imagination free reign. Suppose the present bodily restrictions removed. Suppose a total openness of each to all the others. Suppose the others to be extended to include all without limit. Suppose that still the creative process goes on, the many becoming one and being thus increased by one. The new ones in their turn perish and in dying make possible their successors. Each new momentary experience is ontologically an individual. Also it inherits from the past succession in which it stands. But its individuality is now inclusively social. It inherits also from all the other individuals as well. Soon the particular connectedness to a particular past ceases to matter. Each enjoys an inconceivable richness of values and meanings. It is no longer concerned with a personal future, for the whole future is its future, as the whole past is its past. Each lives from all and for all. In such a future all that matters about our selfhood is preserved, but it is continued, developed, transformed, and purified, passing from the compartmentalized and protected psyche that we now know into myriads of free and open selves unconcerned with their peculiar lines of inheritance.

In these last remarks about both the historical and the supra-historical future, you have been hearing only my own idiosyncratic speculations. I have not been speaking for process theology in general. Most process theologians have been content with Whitehead's own eschatology, centering on the consequent nature of God.

Even so, my speculations are legitimately Whiteheadian. Whitehead envisioned the emergence of new types of societies, and the future community to which I pointed is a possible society. Whitehead recognized also the ontological possibility that high-grade, conscious experiences can occur beyond physical death and apart from human bodies as we know them. Few process theologians have interested themselves in this possibility, but my speculations remain within the process frame.

My concern for some form of ongoing fulfillment independent from the present physical base is heightened by my acute fear that man's time on this planet already draws to an end. Process theology gives me hope that man *can* find his way through the now-threatening catastrophes, but it gives me no assurance that he *will* do so. The fear of a cataclysmic end in the near future increases my sense of the urgency of responsible action now, but it increases also my interest in ways of conceiving a fulfilling future other than continuance or consummation of our earthly history. In this interest I feel quite lonely both among process theologians and among contemporary Christian thinkers generally—sometimes even somewhat ridiculous. But I have not yet found an alternative that is both credible and adequate to sustain Christian hope and joy.

The Future as Our Future:

A Teilhardian Perspective

PHILIP HEFNER

I. THE STARTING POINT

A Teilhardian methodology for approaching the question of the future may be summed up in a sentence that is found in a letter dated 1923:

> the secret . . . lies in managing, with God's help, to perceive the One Element Needful which circulates in all things, which can give itself to us (with its joy and freedom) through any object, provided that object is brought before us by *fidelity* to life, and that it is transformed by *faith* in the divine presence and operation.[1]

The probing of any datum of reality will open for us the meaning of the whole of reality, if that segment is one which we have come upon as a consequence of our seriousness in being responsible to the life that has been given us.

The characteristic mark of a Teilhardian viewpoint is rooted in the fact that it takes its origins from a lifetime of focusing on the geological and paleontological history of planet earth. This viewpoint grows out of an attempt to establish a unified science of the world, positing that "the world of life, taken as a whole, forms a single system bound to the surface of the earth"[2] and that this single system is bound by physical-chemical links to the history of the planet. Out of concentrated attention to this particular segment of reality, which was lifted up in the course of a serious concern for the meaning of this world and human life in it, came the formulation of a hypothesis known as the Law of Complexity-Consciousness (which will be discussed in more detail below). This hypothesis suggested the answer to the question of meaning: What must be the nature of the real if this hypothesis accurately clarifies the datum which I have focused upon? The answer came back: Reality seeks fulfillment of this thrust toward complexity-consciousness; the real with which we have concourse, both within ourselves and without, has a destiny; the future is the fulfillment of that destiny.[3]

In what follows, I will attempt to spell out in detail what this viewpoint implies for our understanding of the future. But it is essential to be clear about this starting point if our conversations are to proceed fruitfully.

The significance and implications of this characteristic starting point deserve more discussion, but at this point we simply note that this methodology lays the basis for understanding why, in our reflection upon the future, we conclude that although the future is determinative for the world, it is intelligible only as the future of the datum to which we have devoted our concentrated attention. The future is intelligible only as *the future or destiny of what is now and has been*. The future is determinative for what has been and is, in that it is relative to its destiny that the meaning of what has been and what is revealed, and it is relative to this destiny that man's action is focused. Any attempt to uncover the meaning of the world and man, as well as the course which action should follow, without reference to their destiny is abortive. At the same time, the future as such has no final and independent autonomy over against what has been and is; "future" and "destiny" lose their intelligibility except as they are conceived to be present to us in the mode of *the future of what we have been and of what we are*. We may personalize this conviction by saying that it makes no sense to ask the meaning of past-present (world and man), to ask after *our own meaning,* apart from reference to our future destiny, while it makes no sense to speak about the future except as it is intelligible to us as our future.

As a consequence, we can speak of a dialectical relationship between future and past-present.* If either element of the dialectic is ignored or collapsed, the remaining element is left empty (contentless) and thus demonic. The dialectic is this: (1) the future is contentless unless it is conceptualized as the future of what has been and is. It stands as sheer thrust and movement and, consequently, pure critique and negation. As such, the future becomes a demonic notion, shattering what is, driving it on mercilessly without respect for the structural and ecological possibilities and limitations of past-present, becoming the agent of its pathological self-negation and self-destruction. (2) The past-present becomes autonomous and thus heteronomous when it is cut off from the future, which is its destiny. Past-present does not possess the resources to sustain this auto-heteronomy apart from the future; it becomes demonic in that it builds a totalitarianism on insufficient depth and meaning. To sum up, it is impossible to understand the future except relative to a deep probing of the past-present of which it *is* the future. It is impossible to understand the past-present (which is the present identity of man and the world) except relative to the future which reveals what it is destined to become.

II. PROBING THE PAST-PRESENT

Everything hinges, therefore, upon our attempt to discern the dynamics of the past-present—the dynamics or structure which will serve as the basis for our analogizing concerning the nature of the future. Since the future cannot be conceived except as the future of

---

*Note that our use of the term "past-present" is in place of the even more cumbersome repetition of "the world and man." It also carries with it the assumption that what the world and man *are now* is largely what they have been up to this very moment; in other words, present identity is constituted by what one has been. Our present remarks indicate that this present identity which is based on the past is incompletely understood except with reference to what it will become.

what we have been and are, our image of the future is inevitably based on *analogy* from what we have been and are. And as is the case with all analogizing, we must delineate precisely the datum that we deem appropriate as the base from which we analogize.

We reject pre-human and non-human forms of matter and life as inappropriate data for analogizing on the grounds that they do not represent the leading edge of development in the world; they are in a sense too much bound to the past to be certain guides to the future of past-present. Preoccupation with what we commonly call "matter," atomic and sub-atomic particles as the datum for analogizing—if it is made autonomous—ultimately proves to be bloodless in its reduction of the whole to its parts, the living to the inanimate. Similarly, we reject cosmic, interstellar evolution as the foundation for analogizing because it cannot take into account precisely that world which is of paramount concern to us, namely, the planets and, in particular, planet earth and the events which transpire on it. The events on this planet are of relative insignificance, a backwater eddy, in the scheme of interstellar evolution, and thus that evolution cannot be the key to understanding the past-present that is of concern to us.

We do select man as the datum from which we analogize, and man in respect to one particular phenomenon—the history of the rise of consciousness. The measure from which we analogize is the dynamics which are revealed in the history of the development of consciousness from its earliest perceptible appearance up to and including man and his society. We are proceeding under the maxim that anthropocentric dangers are countered by the inescapable fact that "the truth of man is the truth of the universe for man, that is to say the truth, pure and simple."[4] Human life is no epiphenomenon, as the approach from matter and from interstellar evolution would postulate, but rather it is the latest and most characteristic term of universal physical-chemical processes. Man

> represents, individually and socially, the most synthesized state under which the stuff of the universe is available to us. Correlatively, he is at present the most mobile point of the stuff in course of transformation.

For these two reasons, to decipher man is essentially to try to find out how the world was made and how it ought to go on making itself.[5]

The evolution of the world itself points to man and his peculiar gifts of consciousness and self-consciousness as the leading edge of evolution, but at the same time, evolution cannot be understood correctly unless it is interpreted in light of man; that is, the circular reasoning in which we are caught. Man is not construed over against the other elements of physical-chemical evolution, but rather as a part of that evolutionary chain, as a phase of it, and indeed as its most recent and complex phase. In this sense, man is the epitome of the evolution of the world; he possesses consciousness and self-consciousness, which in turn are the most recent members in that equation that begins with the first perceptible appearance of consciousness in pre- and non-human forms.

What we discover when we focus on the datum of consciousness, reaching its most recent form in man's self-consciousness, is the Law or Hypothesis of Complexity-Consciousness. Put in its most succinct form, this hypothesis states that the trend of evolution is toward the more complex, and that the most complex configuration of the *Weltstoff* to date is the self-consciousness found in man, not only as an individual, but the self-consciousness that is the intersubjective consciousness of the species in the global village. This trend toward complexity is the Ariadne's thread that lights up the meaning of past-present, from the origins of the earth to the present. The unit of measurement is not the infinitely small nor the infinitely large, but rather complexity. The molecule is more complex than the atom; the cell more complex than the molecule; the organism more complex than the cell; the society more complex than the organism; the self-reflective organism in society more complex than the merely conscious, but unself-conscious.

We can, however, probe the dynamics of this trend toward complexification still more. We find that this trend possesses within it a double rhythm of development: the impulse toward aggregation or simple multiplicity and the impulse toward centeredness or organization of identity. Intensification of both of these—multiplicity plus centeredness—constitutes a trend toward complexity.

The trend toward complexity is a cosmic process, now localized most dynamically in the humanified or hominized phase of the world's development. Geology may have been its first phase; the present global system of civilization set in the context of its physical environment is the ultra-development of the process that was once solely geological. We are speaking in Einsteinian terms: reality is energy under its several configurations. What we commonly call "matter" is the series of events in which energy moves in certain configurations. The present global system of humanified energy is the most complex configuration of energy yet attained, and self-consciousness is its characteristic mark; this energy grows in quantity and multiplicity while also focusing ever more intensely upon its own identity and thus centering itself ever more intensely.

We analogize, therefore, on the basis of this axiom:

> The degree of consciousness attained by living creatures (from the moment, naturally, when it becomes discernible) may be used as a parameter to estimate the direction and speed of Evolution.[6]

The structure assumed by evolving energy thus rests upon three trends: (1) energy incarnates itself in physical development which moves toward (2) unification or multiplicity and (3) centeredness or intensification of identity. The future is the fulfillment of this trend of evolving energy forms, or, to say the same thing, the destiny of man and the world is to fulfill this trend.

III. THE PROBLEM OF THE FUTURE EMERGES—ENERGY-ACTION

Reflection upon the future as the fulfillment of the past-present evolution of the energy which is the *Weltstoff* leads directly to the central issue: human action. Our reflection may be grounded in insights that grow out of a preoccupation with prehistoric developments, geological, biological, and paleontological, and this preoccupation may be coupled with attempts to fashion a total science which can comprehend all of reality, but the issue it raises has to do with the shape and direction of human action—not simply actions of individuals, but also and even more the actions of groups and of the entire species. The energy of the cosmos which tends toward complexification—centered multiplicity—manifests itself there where complexity is most advanced, and this means those areas where activity is constantly heightened.[7] One of the most distinctive properties of life is its response to stimulation and its subsequent action. The most advanced manifestation of life in man is in his self-conscious, reflected upon action. Hence, for Teilhard himself, the most neglected new science that needed to be undertaken was that of energetics, specifically human energetics. Such a discipline of reflection would be centered on one "simple and certain rule"; human action should be guided by the knowledge that evolution means to go in the direction of those possibilities which the universe opens up for action which will advance complexification.

To introduce some explicitly Teilhardian jargon, we are now entering upon the areas delineated by the terms "activance" and "activation." "Activance" refers to the power which a force possesses for developing and stimulating energy into action.[8] Activance subordinates knowing and being to growing, becoming, and acting. This corresponds to Teilhard's vision of evolution as much more than a scientific hypothesis, but rather "an expression of the structural law (both of 'being' and of knowledge) by virtue of which *nothing, absolutely nothing*, we now realize, can enter our lives or our field of vision except by *way of birth* . . . taken in the general sense of 'cosmogenesis,' it represents the only dimensional setting in which our capacity to think, to seek and to create can henceforth function."[9] A philosophy of "genesis" or growing, becoming, and acting must focus ultimately upon human action, first individual and then species, because at its most complex point, the evolution of energy is manifest in the form of a species of life that is not only configured of energy, that is not only responsive to stimuli, but which reflects upon itself, its situation, and its action and therefore is the agent of reflected upon action.

Since this leading edge of the energy which is the real has presently come to reside in human action, Teilhard moved on to the philosophical elaboration that "the real must, again, be, to the highest possible degree and with no limit, *actable* and *activating*. In other words, there would be a contradiction, an ontological imbalance, in the world if our capacity to desire and to act were found to be greater, even in one single point, than the possibilities offered to us by our cosmic environment. . . . In virtue of its structure the world must offer, in relation to our zest for action, a maximum power of stimulation (a maximum *'activance'*). To be merely *actable*, it must be supremely *activating*."[10]

This may sound perniciously anthropocentric and may suggest man's free course to exploit the world around him in the name of his "zest for action." We must keep in mind, however, that we are here speaking of man, not as separate from and over against the world, but rather as a part of the evolution of the *Weltstoff* energy in its many phases, the presently most active and complex configuration of that energy. And since this is so, the problem of action is pre-eminently the problem of man's using his reflective capacity, that is of participating in this energy, so as to discern adequately which are the unlimited capacities for desire and possibilites for action which will fulfill the destiny of the *Weltstoff,* the destiny of the movement toward centeredness and unification. In Teilhard's words:

> . . . *for the first time* since the awakening of life on earth, the fundamental problem of action has finally emerged into our human consciousness in the twentieth century . . . the fundamental matter has become one of rationally assuring the progress of the world of which we form part.[11]

A Teilhardian perspective on the future implies, therefore, a program which: (1) is devoted to a close study of past-present, (2) gives ontological priority to process (or genesis) and action, and (3) entails by necessity an ethical imperative to advance the process. Consequently, the celebrated Teilhardian "optimism" which has been variously interpreted as the strength and the weakness of this perspective, must be very keenly aware of the fact that the future and man's share in it rest on precarious foundations, even though that future is given primary ontological status. The precarious foundation is precisely that dimension which gives distinctiveness to the leading edge of evolution—man's self-consciousness and its reflective capacities. *Will* man's conscious reflection adequately discern the fundamental nature of past-present and thus properly understand what its future is to be? *Will* that reflection understand that it is the future, the destiny of this world which reveals to man his meaning, or will it be devoted to an abortive disruption of the dialectic between past-present and future? If man's reflection does come to terms adequately with these first two issues, *will* individual men and *will* the species have the courage to act in a manner that is obedient to the imperative of the future? Teilhard's optimism stems from his faithfulness to the life he had been given and what he discerned there, under the impact of God's presence and operation, but he was always aware of the fragility of the evolutionary enterprise. I think I see more expressions of this awareness in the small pieces that date from his later years. I read of his concern lest mankind "fall out of love" with its destiny, lest the soul of man "go on strike" against the future of the world's evolution, lest man's spiritual resources and zest for living be depleted before the physical resources about which the conservationists were writing in the 1950's. Whether this is a correct interpretation of Teilhard or not, we do see clearly today the fragility of the foundations on which hope for the future rests.

If the hope is fragile, then the *truth* about the future and its clear and persuasive communication become all the more urgent. The power of the future in our humanified world is human action which advances the fundamental thrust of centered multiplicity which is the world's destiny. For the self-conscious and reflective zone of energy which is the leading edge of evolution and therefore must sustain the presence of the future, clarity of truth is essential. The Teilhardian perspective, once again circular in its reasoning, holds the criterion of truth that statements must be coherent to the proposition that the world has a future and that man's self-conscious action can so advance the fundamental thrust of evolving energy as to move toward that future and thus toward the "success of the universe." The maxim is: "What is the most intelligible and the most activating is necessarily the most real and the most true."[12] In our analogizing about the future, that is a true image or statement which serves to activate to the highest degree, human energy in action which contributes to the fulfillment of the world's destiny.

This stands as a coherence criterion of truth, because it rests on the assumption that human action, human conceptions of the truth, and reality itself must be in consonance with one another. We must comment upon this assumption later in more detail. Here we can only express the conviction that human self-consciousness cannot finally give itself to the action that is responsible to the destiny of this world if it is not convinced that the world does indeed have a destiny that is consonant with the personhood of man and his species, and if it is not clear about that destiny and its structure. Man must not only act, he must be at home in the environment in which he is acting, and he must find that environment "thinkable" or comprehensible. To be at home in the world is to find it in basic consonance with the human enterprise; to find that world comprehensible is to find that the environment is consonant with man's mind as well as with his body and will. The comprehensive notion of coherence which is here set forth is at odds with absurdist positions and nihilist positions, and it rests very largely upon circular arguments, even though it finds its position demonstrable, to its own satisfaction, in the empirical world and places a high premium upon that demonstrability.

IV. SIX BASIC STATEMENTS ABOUT THE FUTURE

A number of large issues have been raised thus far which need further discussion, brief though that may be. I have chosen six for comment here.

A. The Future Is One of Convergence and Unification

The future of man—the future of the energy which is developing through the human species now as its leading edge—is one of continued convergence or unification. A number of physical factors lie at the root of this trend: (1) the apparent converging trend of the human species, which is in contrast to other species of life, but which is an intensification of the pre-human history of consciousness, (2) the spherical shape of the earth, which decrees that a species which becomes fully planetary in breadth, within a global village, will necessarily be an interrelated whole system. After physical, geographical planetization is accomplished—an event which took place sometime within the last one generation (perhaps during World War II?)—new frontiers of unification arise. Unification in quantitative terms builds up the pressure that provides the circumstances under which qualitative changes can occur, the changes that are authentically new. Increased unification of a more densely planetized human species does not simply augur "more of the same," more density, closer communications, etc. Rather it builds up pressures which are the seedbed of the *Novum*, which we can neither predict nor domesticate; we will only be able to say in retrospect that at some point the quantitative developments crossed the line of qualitative alterations.

Teilhard's own personal criticisms of individualism are well known. He reserved the term "individualism" for the headstrong unwillingness to acknowledge the fundamental unity among men, as well as between man and his environment. He used the term to discredit the suggestion that the problems of massed humanity as a planetary species could be avoided through a willful or romantic escape into individual autonomy, just as he rejected the idea that the trend toward collectivization could be turned back. Sometime in the first half of the twentieth century, the human species became a planetary entity and crossed irreversibly over the line where it attained a species consciousness. This consciousness is not yet full-orbed; in fact it has not even taken firm shape on most fronts; but it is in existence, and it cannot be eradicated so long as there is a viable human species.

This postulate of convergence or unification means that the Teilhardian perspective is intrinsically oriented toward the political dimension of human existence, as well as toward the management of technology—in addition to its well-known concern for spirituality and personal development. Furthermore, the postulate of unity rests on the conviction that ultimately our concern for the future must deal with the whole, the totality. The real is ultimately one, the God who undergirds and calls forth the process of evolution is one, the meaning around which all personal centers cluster is one. The concept of the future is totalizing, not fragmenting.

The character of mankind's unity, which is the epitome of the unity of the geosphere and the biosphere also, since the planet is now humanified, needs to be understood in the light of certain clear distinctions. Above all, it is recognized that the collectivization of massed humanity is full of perversions, some of them commonly described in terms of the "anthill society," the world of George Orwell's 1984 and Franz Kafka's Castle, as well as the world of the capitalist corporation. The Teilhardian view bears within it the criticism of such inadequate forms of unification. These forms emphasize only one pole of the trend of evolving energy toward agglomeration. They do not properly understand that the trend of evolution is toward organized or centered multiplicity. The element of centeredness comprises our second statement about the future.

B.   *The Future Is One of Progressive Personalization*

If individualization is the pejorative term, personalization is the positive one. It denotes not just separateness and distinctness, but the intensification of the identity and centeredness which is the inexpressible, precious value of the individual. A Teilhardian perspective brings with it a view of creation and the creative process which is hinted at in the phrases: "Union creates," "union differentiates," "union personalizes."[13] The evolution of energy states is toward a unification of centered entities which do not thereby lose or abandon their individual value, but rather enter into the unity with their personal value intact and thereby enhance it through union. The differentiating and personalizing dimensions are implicit in the Teilhardian concept of union, and it is for this reason that creation can be considered unitive and union creative.

Several considerations must be kept in mind here. Individual value is not to be abandoned or given up into absorption into some greater value—hence Teilhard's own judgment of the inadequacy of Eastern mysticism, as he understood that mysticism. The future cannot be conceived in terms of impersonality, as if to say that the ultimate is a brute force or energy, or a dissipation in terms of Newtonian entropy under the Newtonian interpretation of the Second Law of Thermodynamics. At this point, Teilhard saw himself diverging from the existentialist, Marxist, and Newtonian worldviews. As judged by the criterion of the coherence of truth, these other positions had to be rejected as inadequate or false, and in terms of our topic, inadequate analogies for the future, because they posit a future that is less than the vital center of what man is now, hence they cannot be futures of fulfillment and they would cut the nerve of man's desire to carry out action that will fulfill the trend of evolution. In each of these opposing positions, the challenge arises for us to deal with death. Absorption into the All, stoic resignation in the face of the brute impersonality of the force of energy, participation in the impersonal on-going dialectic of the material, or simply dissipation and dispersion, providing fertilizer for the eons ahead, these are all ways of saying that death finally destroys what is most precious to us, our personhood.

Personalization does not mean that man projects upon the cosmos a great person in his own image, resonating with himself, as an attempt to avoid death's verdict. On the contrary, it means that the factors and forces which are apparent in pre-human and non-human energy configurations, as well as in man, which make for personal identity and value constitute a continuum which shall advance toward intensification, in ways that we cannot foresee, but in ways that are not retrogressive. The future, therefore, will be an intensification of our personhood, and not a dispersion of it.

The unification of which we speak is described as one of harmony and peace, but these terms must be defined with care. Peace is neither "millenary felicity" nor "bourgeois tranquillity."[14] It is the tense cohesion of centered entities who have not been unfaithful to their own identity; the impulse toward centricity remains, and so the peace of union is a complex sublimation of the forces of war and hostility. This dialectical tension dare not be relaxed. It is the dialectical tension which heats up the mass so that the new can come into existence—the new which fulfills all the centered selves.

C. *The Future Is Open, not Closed*

The principle of coherence to which we alluded earlier renders fully unacceptable a conception of the future that is closed, limited, or manipulable. The future must be truly future, which means new and not susceptible to domestication. A Teilhardian perspective calls attention to the open-ended character of evolution; man and the cosmos are still evolving, and this entails qualitatively new developments. The openness of the future is a postulate for man's feeling and thinking himself "at home" in his world, inasmuch as he holds to the unlimited actability and activating character of the world. Again, this may seem to be the statement of Promethean man, bent on unlimited exploitation, unbridled in pride. But as Teilhard himself responded when Gabriel Marcel confronted him on this point, Promethean man is man unreflective—in the sense that he has not gone beyond the consideration of his action to the question of the direction in which his action should tend; Promethean man does not transcend his own actions. The Teilhardian presupposes that the future is open and that the world is limitless in its actability only in certain directions, namely in the direction which leads to the fulfillment or destiny of the evolving *Weltstoff*. Man's task as a reflective zone is to discern that direction and determine his action accordingly, that is, his meaning and evolutionary role. This is not to be construed as crass extrapolation from existing trends, but rather a discernment of the nature and demands of the evolving energy which is the real and a commitment to the future thereby opened up into a limitless and unpredictable realm.

D. The Future Implies the Worth and Reliability of Creation

Underlying much of the foregoing, particularly the affirmation of the openness of the future, is the assumption that the world is reliable, that the evolutionary process in which the energy of *Weltstoff* lives out its career is reliable, is a viable process. If the future is not fulfillment or consummation of the evolutionary process, then it is not the future of this world, it is not *our* future. If the future is catastrophe or if it is fundamentally critique of creation, then it is not *our* future, and furthermore it means that much of what we have believed is false or at least misleading.

This is an assertion that is difficult to express with the proper subtlety. On the one hand, it appears to be a simplistic conviction that there is an irrefragability or invincibility of the created order and its tendency toward fulfillment. This conviction seems to approve whatever is and whatever happens as the irrevocable, if somewhat puzzling, thrust toward the consummation. It seems to overlook evil and trivializes the ambiguities of history and the fragilities of the process of human action. On the other hand, we have been given one life, membership in one species, and participation in one evolutionary process. The only inputs we have for any of our beliefs, insights, or worldviews come from within and through that life, that species, and that evolutionary process. The great task of the human being, and of his species, is to assess the meaning of this life, this species, and this evolutionary process, and to act according to what his reflection upon those inputs tells him. Any position which he or the species adopts assumes, ultimately, that the process in which the reflection has taken place is reliable *and* thus viable, however that reliability and viability are defined and conceptualized. For example, the recent statement by the French Nobel Laureate in biology, Jacques Monod, that life has come about purely by chance, is described by Monod himself as a conclusion which he reached through the strictest objectivity, under the imperative of the "ethics of discernment" which allows for no judgments of value and which has attended only to the rigorous laws and necessities of the evolutionary process. The absurdist position of a Camus asserts that there is no consonance between man's deepest insights into his own needs and the world around him. I understand the theologians of hope in this group to be saying that the future which is God's future stands very largely as critique of the created order, sometimes even in the tones of a Barthian *totaliter*. All of these positions, as different as they may be, rest on the assumption that the process in which they have participated in reaching their conclusions has provided them with reliable inputs. But, as Schubert Ogden has put the issue, must this reliability of inputs not be transposed into the question of the long-range, eternal viability and reliability of the creation? The question of whether the geological, biological, and paleontological evidence of the last several billion years of evolution is reliable is immediately pushed ahead to the consummation in eternity. If the process is reliable enough to draw conclusions about its meaning and its future, even if that conclusion is one of absurdity or one that posits God's future as critique over against man and creation, then the question also arises whether the reliability of the process and the value of the personal dimension which has sustained reflection stops here, whether it is to be authentically consummated or finally dissolved, whether that dissolution is into catastrophe, Newtonian entropized matter, or into a consuming fire of God's future.

A Teilhardian perspective rests on the conviction that the universe (and this includes our world, our species, ourselves) is thinkable, livable, and viable, to be consummated, because it is of absolute worth. The question of evil and defect is very real because the unitive-personalizing process that *is* creation moves through unavoidable pain, misjudgment, willfulness. Man can destroy the process. But if he does, then the strange circularity and paradoxicality in which we must think leads us to say that the entire edifice of thought and belief which we hold will have been proven wrong, and that it will be clear in a twinkling that either God is not or that our understanding of him has been monumentally false. This is to say that our conviction of the reliability and absolute worth of creation is an inexorable postulate both of our reason and of our faith, worked out in fear and trembling, and the two, faith and reason, stand or fall together.

The corollary to this is that the world matters to God; it is not dispensable to him; his transcendence, however that is to be conceived, does not allow that the creation can be demeaned or ultimately allowed to be destroyed. The panentheist proposal obtains here. The world is in God, and this implies that every personal identity or value is irreversible and eternal.

E.   *The Future Activates Human Energy*

The substance of the cosmos is energy and the evolutionary process of events in which energy assumes certain forms; the issue is how the most complex form of this energy, human individual and species energy, can be activated in the direction of fulfilling the process. The image or concept of the future is the activating agency. Pre- and non-human configurations of energy may be activated *a retro*, by determinisms that work upon them externally from behind, a push. But self-conscious and reflective man is activated from ahead, by the unfinished, the unexpected, the ideal. With self-consciousness, the evolutionary process has entered a phase "characterized by an increasing predominance of the effects of fear or hope allied to the formidable gift of foresight."[15]

This accounts, in part, for the insistence that our analogizing about the future be judged by the coherence criterion of truth, coherence with action that contributes to the fulfillment of the world's destiny, because without that coherence, the human energy for action will either go unactivated or be activated wrongly. Analogies of the future which speak of ultimate absurdity, ultimate impersonality, or ultimate absorption into the All—these rank for Teilhard as inadequate activating images. We might ask, also, whether this criterion is reconcilable with a view that speaks of the future as God's future apart from a correlation to the phenomenological requirements that describe *our* future.

The transformation from activation of pre- and non-human energy *a retro* to activation of human energy *from ahead* is a transition of significant proportion, one which Teilhard called the tran-

sition from the "old" to the "new" evolution, not only because it
shifts, so to speak, the motor of evolution from the rear to the
front, but also because that shift is correlated to self-conscious
reflection which must be brought to bear critically in order to discern and make value judgments about the image of the future that
is most real and true.

What is at stake here is a new mode of energizing. The trend is
toward unification through action, but since this unification entails
the utmost intensification of the personal, this energizing is totally
free, in the final analysis, from external compulsion and totally
dependent upon "zest" for the evolutionary process and voluntary
commitment of the advancement of that process toward its fulfillment. This is what we term "spiritual energy"—the energy that is
activated by an image of the future that is true by the criteria we
have mentioned, which means that the image is persuasive enough
to awaken and sustain the zest for life that motivates a strong voluntary commitment to the advancement of the process of evolution.
Fear and desire to survive at the biological level are a part of this
zest and commitment, but increasingly the revolution of rising
expectations signifies that "no longer is there simply . . . the sting
of death to be avoided: there is the passion for outdistancing ourselves and reaching a peak we can glimpse through the clouds."[16]
Coherence entails the concept of the future union of the totality of
centers, the intensification of the personal, and the irreversible
worth of the created order and its process of evolution. Nothing
less than an image of the future that includes these can activate
human energy adequately.

F.   *Love Is the Action which Fulfills the Destiny*

Love is the term which covers the action in which activated
human energy contributes toward the fulfillment of the evolutionary process which at the present time focuses in man. Several distinctions need to be made in order to give more precise content to
the concept of love. First, love is defined as the action of union
between centered persons which is freely entered into. This distinguishes it from coerced action, from union which is tangential,

drawn from peripheral concerns and not a center-to-center union. Second, there is great emphasis placed upon the centering effects of true love. Love gives centeredness or identity to the various actions a person enters into; it gives center to a person's entire life itself; it gives center or identity to a group of persons acting together and thus, theoretically, to all of humanity. Love totalizes at these differ-ent levels, by pulling together and centering. Just as complexifica-tion is union of centers of identity, so love is union of selves who maintain and enhance their centeredness in the union.[17] Third, love is engaged, under all its forms, in world-building—in building up the stuff of our world and our fellow human beings in it—not just on an individual basis, but in ways appropriate to a species that is now planetary in scope and whose challenge is to contribute to the fulfillment of the world. Fourth, this love is by definition earthy and material. World-building is contribution to the physical develop-ment of persons and the world. Love is mercy, politics, psychother-apy, as well as the organization of the energies of the human race.

V. THE TWO FAITHS

The future is the destiny of this world, and our image of that destiny is built on analogy from what we discern in the nature of the past-present reality which we are. This destiny gives meaning to human existence and to the larger evolutionary process of which human existence is a part, and it gives focus to the action which makes concrete the energy of which we are comprised. This mean-ing and focus point us toward the unification of all reality which we enter into freely while maintaining the integrity of our own identity.

Because this conceptuality of the future deals with the evolution-ary process and with the intensification of personal worth and cen-teredness through action, it is by definition · concrete and not abstract. Therefore, it is manifested in concrete sets of symbols, concrete communities with specific histories. Teilhard himself spoke of two kinds of communities concerned with the process of life: those which discerned that destiny is calling man forward, toward the Ahead, and those which discerned that man's life is lived out of an ultimacy, calling man upward toward the Above. The communities of the Ahead were admirable in their courage and their essential correctness in assessing the course of this world's history, but they were too often superficial in their rejection of transcendence or monomaniacal in their commitment to a limited view of the Ahead. These communities were some scientific groups, the Marxists, and some political groups, including Fascists. The communities of the Above were largely the religious communities, most of whom sought to escape the challenges and the newness of the Ahead by recourse to the God who is above this world, and who is the seat of ultimacy. Obviously, stated in this way, neither set of communities is adequate for the human species in the years that lie ahead. The religious communities must recognize that the ultimate reality they know and worship, God, is the God Ahead, not the God Above, and thus they may gain a true insight into God and his will for their own lives and at the same time provide correction and depth for the communities of the Ahead. If the Above is symbolized by the vertical force and the Ahead by the horizontal, then the God Ahead is symbolized by the line of force which is their resultant, proceeding from the point of their intersection at a 45° angle.[18] God, thus, is the "Prime Mover Ahead," the "Mover, Collector, Consolidator, the God-Forward of evolution."[19]

By pointing to the ultimacy of the forward-moving process, the religious community provides meanings through its symbols for what every sensitive person feels and shares in this secular activity. These symbols are concrete, growing out of the specific history of the community. The Christian symbols are the concrete vehicles for understanding the meaning of the process of which we are a part, the direction in which it is going, the shape of our actions. Christ is the Omega toward which the process is tending—ultimate unification of all things, with the most intense personalization of the individual value and identity—and Omega, which is both presence and eschaton, both source and goal, both context and direction. Christ reveals to us that the process is in God, and that his transcendence lies in his being the future of our past-present, rather than in his being distant from our material realm.

VI. CONCLUSION, QUESTIONS

The first set of conclusions to which I draw attention have to do with the Teilhardian starting point for thinking about the future. First of all, defining the future as the fulfillment or the destiny of the past-present carries with it certain implications—that the future is present among us in the mode of being *our future*, that is, the future that fulfills what we have been and thus are, and that therefore the discernment of the fundamental dynamics of past-present is essential if we are to discern and obey the future. Second, this raises the question as to precisely what is meant by the growing terminology that speaks of eschatology versus teleology, *adventus* versus *futurum*, eschatology versus extrapolation. I understand these sets of antinomies to be attempts to underscore the point that the future cannot be deduced from the past by simplistic extrapolation of trends, and therefore the future cannot be manipulated and domesticated; proper attention is thereby given to the genuinely new. This intention is certainly validated by now. On the other hand, assertions that speak of the future coming at us, breaking in as eschatology rather than as teleology (which traces an unfolding of the future from the past) can be and have been misleading if they make it difficult to conceptualize the future as our future, the destiny of past-present. We may indeed be uncomfortable with attempts to domesticate the future through crass extrapolation. Furthermore, the past is so full of horrors that we must recognize that the future exercises critique upon it. But the future is the future of the past which we have been given, and we must guard against the twin attempts to make the future so sovereign that we cannot enter into its dynamics, on the one hand, and to make the future sheer critique, on the other. The statement that the future is God's future, over which he has dominion, must not collapse the polar statement that it is man's future for which he is responsible; similarly, the vision of future as critique of the past and present cannot be allowed to collapse the polar vision that the future is the substance upon which we build, the power of what we will be. The concept of the future can become an instrument of self-negation and even masochism, if it is allowed to be totally sovereign or wholly critique. I would prefer to say that the future does not call us to reject the past so much as to come to terms with the past; when we say that we decide against the past, we really mean that we decided that the future may not be permitted to repeat or reinforce the pathology of the past. For example, the German past contains a Dachau, the American past a Vietnam and decades of racism, which means that in a sense the German future is forever Nazified and the American future is forever Vietnamized and racified. The question is what is the future of that Germany and that America, and when we say rhetorically that we have rejected Dachau and Vietnam and racism, we actually mean that we have chosen to work for certain futures rather than others.

A second set of conclusions follow directly upon the first, namely, a correlation between a Teilhardian perspective and the phenomenology of Heidegger, Merleau-Ponty, Ricoeur, Gibson Winter, and others. I believe that this correlation is essential. To say that the mode of the future's presence among us is as *our future* is to say that Heidegger and Winter, for example, are essentially correct in describing the dynamics of our futuring in terms of the project, the projection (*Entwurf*, not *Projektion*), the casting forth of the future of what we have been within the structures of the present. The complex, but clear, analysis which these men have set forth accurately describes how the the future is realized as the mode of the past's authentic projection under the circumstances of the present. The problems which many have uncovered in Heidegger's tendency toward the privatization of futuricity have been overcome, in my opinion, when this phenomenological description is linked to an objective metaphysics (of Teilhard, Whitehead, Hartshorne, or Hegel) and to the social and corporate structures of human existence as Winter (building upon Schuetz and Mead) does in his phenomenology of policy. The phenomenologists must be included in any discussion of the future because their work is essential if we are to understand how the future destiny to which we give ontological priority and transcendent divinity enters into the dynamics of our human existence. Without their work it is much more difficult to understand the mode of the future's presence.

Third, there are conclusions which deal with the fundamental assumption *that the created order is trustworthy, viable, and of absolute worth*. This assumption seems offensive to many in these days when the fallibility and perversity of men and the vulnerability of nature are so obvious. Nevertheless, the question pushes us still deeper to probe what it might mean to deny the viability and trustworthiness of creation—whether in the name of absurdity or in the name of God's sovereignty. To affirm the trustworthiness of the created order may be closer to Schubert Ogden's position, that an atheism which denies this trustworthiness is ultimately impossible, than it is to the position that God's future is sovereign, and that that future will hold even if this world goes up in smoke. The God question *is* the question of the reliability of the creation order, and it is difficult to speak of the future or of God apart from that reliability. The question of evil is another matter that obviously comes into focus here, but it is too monumental and complex even to touch upon.

Finally, there are implications which arise from the assertion that the question of the future is fundamentally the question of activating the *human energy available*, together with the energy of man's natural support system, so as to advance evolution toward its fulfillment. As vague as this may seem, it is precise enough to lay before us the challenge of: (1) organizing and mobilizing human energy, so as (2) to accomplish the unification of the human mass within its global environment, while (3) at the same time intensifying the personal centeredness and identity of every individual and group within the planetized mass, and (4) recognizing that this mobilizing of energy toward these ends is simultaneously the pathway toward ultimacy, God. The genuinely *political* and the genuinely *religious* are brought together. *Homo politicus* must be at the same time *homo religiosus* at least for a Teilhardian. The political task, if it is properly conceived, is an encounter with the numinous. The numinous encounter is indissolubly linked to the enterprises of the technical assessment and political organization of physical and spiritual energy, as well as to the whole range of ethical reflection.

When the Teilhardian perspective is viewed in this manner, it is risk and wager as much as it is optimism. Our talk about the future is the obverse side of our confidence that man does have a destiny and our hope that he can realize that destiny. A Teilhardian recognizes that that destiny is God's future in Jesus Christ, but he also believes that the traces of God's will and action up to now in the evolutionary process which God created indicate that God has so incarnated himself and his future into the dynamics of the self-conscious zone of his creation that the future of the cosmos and of God rests upon man—man can kill himself, his world, and God. That is why the activation of man's energy is the crucial question of the future, because if that energy is not activated in the proper direction, we will be only moments away from the abyss, and whether our belief has been right or wrong all these centuries, we will in any case be without men or God.

NOTES

All references are to the writings of Pierre Teilhard de Chardin.

[1]*Letters to Léontine Zanta*, tr. Bernard Wall (New York: Harper & Row, 1969), p. 50.

[2]"Géobiolgie et Geobiologia," *Geobiologia*, 1 (1943), 1; quoted in Claude Cuénot, *Teilhard de Chardin: A Biographical Study*, tr. Vincent Colimore (Baltimore: Helicon, 1965), p. 228.

[3]Cf. *The Phenomenon of Man*, revised English edition (New York: Harper & Row, 1965), pp. 47ff.

[4]*Human Energy*, tr. J. M. Cohen (New York: Harcourt Brace Jovanovich, 1971), p. 55.

[5]*The Phenomenon of Man*, pp. 281-282.

[6]*The Future of Man,* tr. Norman Denny (New York: Harper & Row, 1964), p. 218.

[7]*Science & Christ,* tr. René Hague (New York: Harper & Row, 1968), p. 172.

[8]*Ibid.,* p. 171.

[9]*Activation of Energy,* tr. René Hague (New York: Harcourt Brace Jovanovich, 1971), pp. 272-273.

[10]*Science & Christ,* pp. 174-175.

[11]*Human Energy,* p. 124.

[12]*Science & Christ,* p. 175.

[13]*Activation of Energy,* pp. 115-117.

[14]Cf. *The Future of Man,* p. 153.

[15]*Activation of Energy,* p. 366.

[16]*Ibid.,* p. 367.

[17]*Human Energy,* pp. 146-155.

[18]*The Future of Man,* p. 269.

[19]*La Place de l'homme dans la nature* (Paris: Seuil, 1963), p. 173. English translation by George Shriver, in his translation of Georges Crespy, *From Science to Theology: An Essay on Teilhard de Chardin* (Nashville: Abingdon, 1969), p. 74.

The Significance of the Future:

An Eschatological Perspective

CARL E. BRAATEN

The theme of the future is both fascinating and frustrating. Someone was asked—I don't remember who—why he was so enchanted by the future. He replied, "That's where I plan to spend the rest of my life." The as-yet-unknown arouses fascination! But the theme of the future is also frustrating because prophecy is its proper medium. As the Chinese proverb says, "To prophesy is extremely difficult—especially with respect to the future." I am no prophet. Nevertheless, I intend to present and support the thesis that man and the culture of which he is a member have a consciousness of the future that expresses itself through its dominant symbols and myths, and that these in turn hold the key to "what lies hidden in the lap of the gods." I think it is possible to develop this thesis in terms of a general philosophy of man and society, as well as in terms of a specifically Christian theology of existence and history. The reasons of the heart (Pascal) are still reasons that must be understood with respect to concrete personal and social experience. So for the purposes of this paper I am not going to strain to segregate philosophical and theological arguments, but to let them freely intermingle according to the subject matter.

I. CONSCIOUSNESS OF THE FUTURE

Future consciousness is grounded in the fundamental experience of man in history. The awareness of the distinction between what has happened in time and what has not yet happened comes to the surface in the process of the self reflecting on itself and its world of experience. "What has not yet happened" is the stuff of the future; its difference from the present and the past is portrayed by symbols whose "truth" cannot be measured by correspondence to the empirically observable state of affairs. The truth of the future enshrined in images is of another dimension. This other dimension can be variously depicted by the imagination, that is, by the mind making images of the future. As the self lives in the present between the past that is already and the future that is not yet, it may be appropriate to speak with R. D. Laing of "the divided self." F. L. Polak speaks of the "the split man," pointing to this capacity of the mind to divide its perceptions between this world that already exists here and now and the coming realm of the future. Because of the overdose of psychoanalytic meaning attached to the concept of "the split man," we would prefer to speak of man's duality, his double-wittedness, his capacity to transcend himself and his world by converting his future into the present. Man could not be a spiritual and moral creature without this power of the mind to split open the horizon of experience, revealing the difference and the distance between what is and should not be and what is not yet but ought to be.

The symbols that bear the freight of the future project another realm, so that from the vantage point of the present moment it appears so utterly different, so antithetical, that language erupts into speaking about a totally other world, somewhere beyond this world, or sometime hereafter. If these symbols should be reified and objectified, that is, if they be literalized, then we have a dualism of two extant worlds existing side by side, or one above the other, or one after the other. Then the future would be void of contact with the present; then it would fail to release the power to change the existing state of affairs. But the significance of the future lies in its relation to the present, so that the symbols of eternal life and the hereafter, or of the beyond and the transcendent, or of heaven and the kingdom of God, speak eloquent messages concerning the lack in the present and generate the energies of hope and courage to work for change. These symbols speak of the divine in contrast to the human; they strike into the heart of man and awaken his conscience; they picture a future which lacks all the bad news we hear in the present.

Symbolism is thus the bridge language between the two worlds of which man is a citizen—this world that has already come to pass and the coming world that hopefully will make up for its deficiencies. No one hopes that the future will bring more misery, prolong the pain, and diminish the human potential. Rather, the symbolism of the future enshrines a hope that this imperfect world will not continue this way forever, that the longing for perfection will be realized, that the struggles of this life will have a happy ending, that the Yin phase will be overtaken by the Yang phase in the alternating rhythms of nature and history. If the conviction hardens that the promising symbols of the future will go empty, forever unfilled by solid reality, it would perhaps be impossible to quell the feeling that life so confined to the prison of the present is meaningless or intolerable. It is the function of the symbolism of the future to revolt against the hard-nosed realism that accepts this world "as it was in the beginning, is now, and ever shall be. Amen." In the end, however, this realism is unable to keep its grip on the present, because in snuffing out the life of the symbols, it is forced to retreat in face of a backfiring future that promises only the certainty of death. Realism is only a shade away from nihilism when the future is contracted into a one-dimensional present that stretches backward and forward along an infinite time-scale. For beyond the being unto death that we now experience there is nothing. And the prospect of nothing has no power to generate hope.

What is true of man applies also to the cultural epoch of which he is a part. Cultures rise and fall according to their ability to respond to the challenge of the future. The forces that determine what a society is and what it becomes are not only those that push from the past, but also those that pull from the not-yet-existing future. How can we think of the influence of the future in determining the present? Out of an infinite number of possibilities, the shape of the future begins to emerge in pictorial images. As a rule it is a small minority of creative people—phophets, poets, artists, etc.—who pick up the signals of the future and decode the messages that are being transmitted. The masses in a society, the general public, live from what they can borrow from the original recipients of the revelation from the future. Figures like Moses, Isaiah, and Jesus, or like Augustine, Luther, and Hegel are not furnished to every generation. There are seasons when prophecy dries up and the meaning of the times becomes blurred. The light of the future is eclipsed and the people grope around in the darkness at noon.

The symbolism of the future has social significance because of its double charge; it is dynamite in the present and dynamism toward the future. It mediates a word of judgment on the present and a vision of hope for the future. There are some general characteristics of the nature of this symbolism and its functional aspects that can be roughly delineated.

The symbolism of the future depicts the promised land of plenty or the true homeland of the exiles. It sets goals worthy of human hope and directions for active striving. Whenever there occurs a basic shift in the future hoped for, there will appear corresponding structural shifts in society. In *Ideology and Utopia* Karl Mannheim has shown that the utopian image of the world has formed the greatest force of social propulsion in history. The upwardly mobile classes are pulled ahead by their prospects for the future; the ruling classes are inclined to stand still because of their interests in the present.

The symbolism of the future comes to us in two forms of consciousness—the utopian and the eschatological. The utopian future is projected as another time *in* history; the eschatological future deals with the final fulfillment end *of* history. It has been customary in theology to stress the differences between eschatological and utopian future consciousness, but here we would at first look at some of their overlapping features. Both types of orientation to the future project a picture which represents an about-face of society. The *perverse* elements in human social experience are put into *reverse* so that the world can go forward to a more fulfilling destiny. The root of revolutionary hope lies in the soil of the imagination which can nourish the dreams of a better world to come. The utopian dream is but the eschatological vision come down to earth. But both of them put themselves at a distance from the existing state of the world. They appear radical because they expect a sharp break with the status quo; or they may appear ludicrous because they portray an impossible future too far beyond the boundaries of the present.

At this point it is relevant to acknowledge that the vision of the impossible future can be a tricky mental device to leave the world as it is. But it can also be linked to the sequence of historical events. It can be like an advance scout, dashing ahead of the troops, but then coming back to show them the way. The vision of the future is the motor for change in society, a kind of prime mover always in motion. A society becomes stagnant without the dual service of the futurist vision. The picture of the future is a double exposure; it exposes what is negative in the actual present and what is positive in the desirable future. In calling for repentance, it does not leave men to squirm in the ugliness and wretchedness of the present; it offers them a promise of salvation, lifting their eyes to unprecedented heights of experience. It converts past failures into new beginnings; it does not say die; it moves from critical penetration of the present into visionary preconstruction of the future. "Where there is no vision, the people perish." (Prov. 29:18)

The vitalities are conditioned by the vision of the future in which it mirrors its lacks and its hopes. A culture is headed for decline when its future is wound up so tightly into its present that its mainspring snaps. This is a metaphor to express what Marcuse means by the one-dimensionality of our society. The future must possess qualities of transcendence to free society from the oppres-

sive bonds of its own actuality. The reigning powers of the present
can be broken by a counterattack from the future. The *élan vital* of
cultural history emanates from its operative goals. The open future,
the new world that is not yet, already operates in the present,
taking shape proleptically in the liberated consciousness, and the
symbols of this consciousness in turn stretch forward to embrace
the future that ceaselessly strives to make all things new. When the
future is nothing more than a rehash of the present, when tomorrow is flattened out on the anvil of today, then a sense of future-
lessness begins the process of cultural decline and decay. It could
be that we are talking about *Amerika*–1984, not so far away.

II. THE ESCHATOLOGICAL FUTURE

So far we have been speaking of the meaning of the future that
can be derived from the symbolism of the future that the utopian
and eschatological consciousness project. The distinctions between
them are not always easy to detect. In the same writing, in the
same thinker, symbols that point to a new future in history lie
alongside of symbols that point to a final future of history. Perhaps
without attaining a clear concept of the dialectical relations
between the future in history and the future of history, most of
them implicitly imagined with Thomas Münzer that at the ripe time
"earthly life may swerve into Heaven." The millenium, that is, the
utopia in the future, will open into a future which never stops,
which is eternally coming. Eternity is not the deadend of history,
but the fulfilling horizon of history. How to think of an eternity
that is not the static end of history, but the revolution against every
stasis, always itself moving and open, is a riddle which cannot be
solved by analyzing the symbolism of the future. It is a problem of
philosophical theology that has blown the minds of even great
thinkers.

I do not believe that modern theology, for all its explorations
into biblical eschatology and the eschatology of Jesus, has developed an adequate doctrine of the internal relations between the
future in history and the future of history, that is, between utopia

and eschatology. Modern theology has used eschatology as the coin of the realm, and in all too facile a manner has dismissed utopia and the doctrine of progress as forgeries. Ultimately, it may be that utopia and eschatology have to go their separate ways. Humanism may thrive on utopia, but Christianity dies without eschatology. I would rather think, however, that utopia craves eschatology, that humanism longs for its fulfillment in Christianity. Therefore, beyond the general and undifferentiated way in which we have been speaking of the symbolism of the future, it is necessary to specify the meaning of the eschatological future. Such a specification is at the same the answer to the question about the essence of Christianity. Barth has been quoted a thousand times, so once more won't hurt, to the effect that "Christianity that is not entirely and altogether eschatology has entirely and altogether nothing to do with Christ."[1]

Whatever Barth might have meant by eschatology, we take it to embrace the Christian doctrine of the future. Recently so much has been written just about this subject that almost anything we say in a few words will appear superfluous and less than adequate. But we can offer a few suggestions, first dealing with the subject of biblical eschatology in general, and secondly with the eschatology of Jesus, in particular.

Biblical religion was driven into world history by the force of its belief in the future. At the core of the covenant between Jahweh and Israel and at the base of the new covenant in Jesus Christ is a series of promises that declare the coming of God and of his fulfilling future in glory. What God has done in the past is to make promises that will be kept in the future. Israel is a prime example of the dualistic consciousness which can see the old world for what it is and trust the promise of a new one to come. Promise always refers to the future. The future is present as promise; the promise is the future as word-event in history. Israel lived in the tragedy of the present toward the triumph of the future in God. God is the person of the future at work in historical time to transform the world into new reality.

In Israel's future consciousness there is an intermingling of utopian and eschatological hopes. Beginning with the hope for a future paradise on earth, for the land of promise flowing with milk and honey, she escalates her hope to the magnitude of a new heaven and a new earth. This process in Israel's consciousness that exhibits the self-transcending dynamics of hope, from the particular to the universal, from the material to the spiritual, from the national to the supra-national, from the earthly to the cosmic, from the this-worldly to the other-worldly destiny of all things, has been traced out by many scholars. The one unifying thread throughout this development is the power and promise of the future that keeps Israel moving forward toward ever more universal goals. The most persistent trend is toward the totalization of hope, until in apocalypticism, the stage is prepared for the advent of the absolute future in an historical event, expressed in the Christian confession that Jesus of Nazareth is the self-revelation of God and, indeed, "very God of very God."

It has become very difficult to speak of the eschatological future that has arrived in Jesus of Nazareth without taking up a position *vis-à-vis* all the competing scholarly opinions on the subject of Jesus and the kingdom of God. The fact, however, that the preaching of the historical Jesus has enjoyed the focus of attention in recent years is a sign that Christian theology continues to demand that the truth of its doctrine be measured with reference to what really happened in and through Jesus of Nazareth. What we mean by the future is linked to the relation of Jesus to the future of God. This is the christological problem! Jesus preached the kingdom of God as decisive power advancing toward the present from the future. Jesus did not speak of the future as such; but he looked to the horizon of the future for the inbreaking rule of God in power and glory, and called for repentance, faith and a relation to his person as means of getting ready for the coming of the kingdom. The kingdom of God is future for Jesus, very near but not quite here.

Perhaps we should speak of Jesus' eschatology as *adventology*, in contrast to *futurology,* to make clear that there are two ways to think of the relation of the future to the present. Johannes Weiss made the point against A. Ritschl's theology of the Kingdom that when Jesus prayed, "Thy kingdom come," he did not mean, "may thy kingdom grow."[2] Similarly, Bultmann acknowledges that in Jesus' preaching the "future and present are not related in the sense that the Kingdom begins as a historical fact in the present and achieves its fulfillment in the future. . . . Rather, the Kingdom of God is genuinely future, because it is not a metaphysical entity or condition, but the future action of God."[3] Bultmann contrasts this view to an immanental evolutionary teleological view of the future: "The intrusion of the Hellenistic idea of development into the views of Jesus is especially conspicuous when the Kingdom is called the consummation of the creation, so that an ascending line is drawn from the beginning to the end. In that case the Kingdom would be already present in germ in the creation, and the Kingdom would be the unfolding of these potentialities. Then ideally the Kingdom would already exist in the present, and its purely future character would be destroyed. But there can be no doubt that according to Jesus' thought the Kingdom is the marvellous, new, wholly other, the opposite of everything present."[4]

Weiss was aware that Jesus' idea of the kingdom presents special problems for modern theology, which in various ways has tried to make it something immanent in the world. Thus, Harnack said that what was essential in Jesus' teaching was God's rule in the hearts of men; Rauschenbusch saw it in terms of social progress; C. H. Dodd locates the kingdom for us in the eucharist; Bultmann makes it the kerygmatic impact triggering the crisis of decision in each moment. They and many others have tried to capture the essence of Jesus' idea of the kingdom in terms meaningful to us today. But in doing so they all tended to defuturize and detranscendentalize the kingdom. Perhaps today we are more inclined to retain the elements of futurity as fundamental to the power of the kingdom. Jesus thought and spoke of the kingdom of God as a coming event, and not as an ontological dimension of the world in the process of becoming. We shall try to find words to speak of the futurity of the future as the source of its impact on the present. For in Jesus' preaching the present is the target of the coming kingdom. The future is all about the present; therefore, eschatology in the New Testament always presses home its meaning in terms of concrete ethics.

Johannes Weiss proposed that modern theology should continue to retain the concept kingdom of God as its characteristic watchword, only it should admit that it is using the term in a different sense from Jesus. However, if the sense is *completely* different, the question arises: why retain it as the central watchword? It would be better to find a way to capitalize on Jesus' futuristic eschatological outlook, rather than to employ one hermeneutical *tour de force* after the other to dismiss it as only marginal or non-essential in Jesus' own mind. It would be better to have an understanding of the future that does justice both to the symbolism of the future that illuminates human existence and the history of culture and the futuristic beliefs of Jesus of Nazareth. I am hoping that another chapter in the history of eschatology can be added by this theological generation through the theology of the future it creates. I think this is important both for cultural and churchly renewal.

III. THE REFUTURIZING OF LIFE

The challenge to theology today is to participate in the futurizing of life both within the church and its enveloping culture. The eschatological future is not without a kind of pragmatic verification; one can weigh it and opt in its favor with a view to the practical differences it makes. Eschatology without an ethics of change and a missionary praxis to accompany it would hardly be in line with the achievement of Jesus and the apostolic church. Church history tells us how the eschatological future hope translated itself into history in primitive Christianity. Precisely how such hope can express itself in the present world situation is a matter still up for grabs. We can try to imagine some of its possibilities.

The future gives rise to hope that a great reversal in the present can come about. There is something pathologically morbid in the

Western soul which gulps down revolting novels about the future, and is incapable of projecting a future that is really inviting and worthy of the human adventure. The nightmares we dream follow after us in our waking hours. We are really frightened by our proximity to *Brave New World* and *Animal Farm*. The trends seem to point that way. However, the impact of the eschatological future in the present can, we hope, reverse the trends and start new ones. That only happens through the remnant of those who keep the live coals of hope burning beneath the ashes of despair and defeatism. As for the rest, what Alvin Toffler calls "future shock" makes them content to retreat to the present, glad for every security in the world as they've known it, no matter how grey and drab it might happen to be.

The refusal to capitulate to the trends may seem unrealistic. Would it not be better to cooperate? To play along with the system, knowing that things aren't going to change anyway? The Preacher says, "There's nothing new under the sun." The French say, "The more things change, the more they remain the same." Is this wisdom, or only a cynical apology of the status quo? The odds appear stacked in their favor, but is there no one to bet on a long shot? Could it not possibly be that the future of history is not trapped by immutable laws of nature? In other words, is there a transcendency of the future in God that does not exhaust itself in the "law and order" of this world, so that we can hope for what we do not yet see, do not see how it can be—that this world can be turned upside down, that its negativities can be negated, and that life power can commute the sentence of eternal death? That's the way it ought to be! So let it be! And it can only be if God, the author and source of life, is himself the essential future of everyman and everything that exists, if the future of death which awaits us all is swallowed up in the victory of resurrection through our Lord Jesus Christ. (I Cor. 15:54-57)

The common view is that we take the present situation as the point of departure, so that the future is a prolongation of the present. The Christian view involves an axiomatic reversal in which the new reality is the starting point, so that the future of life becomes retroactively operative in our death-oriented present. The futurizing of life is proclaiming the victory to the spirits in prison, making participation in the new reality a possibility here and now through faith, hope, and love. The benefits of the future which Christ has pioneered need not be postponed to the parousia. This point would have to be developed further in terms of an interpretation of the traditional doctrine of the "real presence."

There is a countercultural dimension of the eschatological future that attacks the "spirit of the times" embodied in the dominant institutions of contemporary society. Our culture is under the spell of a monism, a unidimensional system of thinking, which manifests itself in terms of its priorities: accumulation of objects rather than communication between subjects, amassing of facts with value-free techniques of measurement, analyzing parts without a sense of the whole, speaking erudite words in the indicative, but stuttering when it comes to the imperative, turning the national effort to mathematics and the empirical sciences, and turning off ethics and metaphysics. We are now in the third age which Comte celebrated, beyond mythology and metaphysics, and well into the positivism of science. What is non-scientific is non-existent and a lot of foolishness. What can be seen, measured and controlled has the highest possible value. It is a world in which it is becoming increasingly dangerous for human beings to live.

The real question has to do with humanization. Does the one-dimensional positivism of our educational and communications systems provide a more human milieu than the two-dimensional thinking of eschatology? Positivism leads to the devaluation of all values.

Eschatology fights for the transvaluation of all values. The drive in man to raise himself to the highest values becomes smothered in a world that replaces its theological future with a technological present. It opts for the bird in the hand, rather than the two in the bush. A future without God grants humanity no hope of being set free of the "sufferings of this present time" and "of its bondage to decay." (Rom. 8:18, 21) Dehumanization is enhanced by the loss of belief that anything can be done to bring about a redeeming alternative to the deadly forces that now control man's fate. I believe that demonic forces driving to decadence, destruction, and death are aided and abetted by the eclipse of the glorious future that God has in store for mankind. The resurrection of a positive symbolism of the future is essential, I think, to cultural renewal. Otherwise future-neurosis eats away the collective will to live creatively in spite of the evils we see within and around us.

Perhaps it is time to admit, as in the story about the emperor's new clothes, that for all the talk about eschatology in the history of modern theology, the theological mind has denuded itself of any symbols of the future that can inspire hope and action. The so-called sects preach an other-worldly salvation in grotesque terms, giving theology an easy excuse not to bother about the future. This kenosis of the future impoverishes the language of hope, so that it seems that "we do not know *what* we hope, but only *that* we hope."[5] To salvage what it could of primitive Christian eschatology, modern theology felt it had to give up the symbolism of the future. There are various ways to rationalize this maneuver, such as saying, "After all, the future symbolism is only part of the husk, not the kernel of the gospel." Or saying, "Jesus and the early Christians expected the Kingdom to come in their lifetime, and since it didn't, they were proved wrong. So we can dismiss their unrealized hopes as a mistake." Now the way is prepared to get rid of all the incriminating symbolism of the future, making it all the more easy for Christianity to settle down in her comfortable bourgeoisified culture. For the countercultural impulses of Christianity, empowering her to go against the stream when necessary, emanate from the apocalyptic futurism of the gospel. This is to be found in Jesus, Paul, Luke, and John's *Revelation*. Take the future out of the gospel, and you take the scandal out of Christianity. For the scandal of the gospel was not that a good man died on the cross; many good men had died on the cross. Rather, it was that this crucified man carries the hope of the world, now and forever. Martin

Luther King did not inspire his people to courageous hope because he talked realistically about jobs, better housing, and integrated education but because he could fill his words and imperatives with the double explosive of future symbolism—of dynamite in the present, dynamism toward the future. The religious socialism of the Blumhardts and Ragaz, and still living in the early Tillich, owed its virility to the eschatological concept of the kingdom of God. Tillich became disappointed when the kairos did not come, and began instead to prophesy a sacred void. But man cannot live in a void. Something will rush in to fill it up—angels or demons, that is, images of hope or isms of despair and nothingness.

How can there be today a *resourcement* of the eschatological images of the future? We can hardly remain satisfied with the traditional devices of metaphysics and mysticism, either to throw the future back into the past or to absorb it into a timeless eternity. Nor are we any more successful in believing in a realized eschatology in this world of damnation or in the church, for that matter, unless we spiritualize it out of sight. If the kingdom of the future were already realized, then we would have no need for symbols; we would have the reality itself; and history should have come to a stop. But we still live in need of the symbols; we still live in history; the future is still outstanding, as well as the freedom and the fulfillment ultimately so essential to human hope. The Jewish-Christian movement is the alma mater of this hope, and its milieu is the apocalyptic eschatological symbolism. When this symbolism collapses, faith in God itself crumbles. First, the process of defuturizing eschatology and secondly the process of de-eschatologizing theology paved the way for the "death of God," not only as a cultural phenomenon but also as a theological event. So I am saying, the problem of the future is a theological problem. Ultimately, what we mean by the future is what we mean by God. For God is our Future, the fulfilling power of the future of all things. If the symbolism of the future which holds the hope for a radical transformation of this world and its people into a new world and a new humanity is eliminated from the consciousness of mankind, then the medium of God-language is also destroyed. For God is always introduced in human language as one who will make the difference, bringing another dimension and doing a new thing.

Ebeling has some fine words for it: "Faith confesses that God is the future. . . . If you confess God as the future, then the future becomes quite different, even though and just because you have the same future before you as everyone else of your time. Faith creates a new and true future, in that while enduring this human, all too human, future, it praises God as *the* future, and so transforms the face of this human future."[6]

NOTES

[1]Karl Barth, *The Epistle to the Romans,* tr. Edwyn C. Hoskyns (New York: Oxford University Press, 1933), p. 314.

[2]Johannes Weiss, *Jesus' Proclamation of the Kingdom of God*, tr. Richard H. Hiers and David L. Holland (Philadelphia: Fortress Press, 1971), p. 73.

[3]Rudolf Bultmann, *Jesus and the Word,* tr. Louise P. Smith and Erminie H. Lantero (New York: Charles Scribner's Sons, 1934), p. 51.

[4]*Ibid.,* pp. 158-159.

[5]A quotation attributed to Luther that Bultmann likes to repeat to support his own emptying of the contents of eschatological hope through demythologization and existentialist interpretation.

[6]Gerhard Ebeling, *The Nature of Faith,* tr. Ronald Gregor Smith (Philadelphia: Muhlenberg Press, 1961), p. 181.

Response to
The Opening Presentations

JÜRGEN MOLTMANN

[Editor's Note: After the opening presentations by Cobb, Hefner, and Braaten, responses were given by Moltmann, Pannenberg, and Metz, to whom the three opening speakers responded in turn. It was impossible to include all of these responses in the present volume. We have, however, included Jürgen Moltmann's response, which raised issues that became a significant part of the conference and were discussed in the working sessions of specialists. Cf. above pp. x-xi.]

The first response should clarify the points of our further discussion. In order to speak as clearly as possible I shall try to leave behind politeness. The future of which I wish to speak is not the future thus far referred to in the context of our conference, except in the last part of Carl Braaten's paper. The religious hopes here expressed are not my hopes. The purely speculative expression of hope we have heard so far is not the expression I am concerned with.

(1) Our theories of hope and the future must be self-critical. As I understand it, our theme is supposed to be: What do you mean by the future? This is not my first question, however. My main question is: *Whose* future do you mean? *Cui bono*? Whose hopes are we giving an account of? Phil Hefner said that theological talk about the future must be concerned with the future of *this* world. In concrete terms we speak of the "first world," the "second world," and the "third world"; and their hopes are very different. Is this world really "a global village?" Separation, oppression, ghettos, apartheid, etc. characterize the face of the world. Tübingen and New York may be considered as one global village, but not East Berlin and West Berlin, not North and South Korea, not the USA and Latin America, and perhaps not even East Harlem and this place. Pure theorizing about the future is, obviously, *pure* theorizing and thus abstract. We often talk in abstract terms when we have something

to hide. I am asking for a *critical* theory of hope. Take a good look around! Among the speakers of our conference *I* have seen only whites so far. Thus for many others we probably will be speaking about the *white future,* the future of whites. Take another good look around! Among the direct participants *I* see only representatives of the rich nations and peoples—myself included. Thus we probably will be speaking about the hopes of the affluent, technologically developed nations, and of the entrepreneurs, theological entrepreneurs included. Our attention has been called to the religion of the human "self" in the world process, that is, concretely and critically we presumably spoke of the white self, the capitalist self, of the American and the European in the process of *his* world. Next we'll probably go on to *extrapolate his* future and speak of science and scientific knowledge to which religion must adjust in order to satisfy scientific reason. Liberal theologians of the white bourgeoisie have always talked that way. They overlooked that their concrete starting point was involved in institutional oppression of their neighbors. They spared no effort in making theology scientific and their dialogue with other sciences equally scientific, while overlooking the social and political context of science and of their own theologies. I have the feeling that we white, middle class, and rich theologians are all "color-blind" and prisoners of our own systems. No wonder that others no longer believe our glamorous themes, as, for example, "Hope and the Future of Man." What about the concrete dilemmas of man that should be part of our concerns? As a German I have not the right to say it, but for instance, how does our theme relate to the prisoners of Attica and the poem of Claude McKay they passed around among themselves:

> If we must die, let it not be like hogs,
> Hunted and penned in an unglorious spot,
> While round us bark the mad and hungry dogs
> Making their mock at our accursed lot.

(2) Liberal theology no longer grips me. Only *liberation theology* is for me a theology which radically focuses on Christian hope, as it has been proposed in this country by James H. Cone and Fred-

erick Herzog. Here the future of God and the future of the humanity of man begin in the transforming thought *of the present*. Without *metanoia* no hope. Without transformation of the inhuman system in which we white, rich peoples are imprisoned as the producers of the misery of others, there will be no future which could reasonably be related to God and the humanity of man. A future which will look different from the present and really be new must begin with the *liberation* of man from the present inhuman conditions. Otherwise it will only be a transposition of the inhuman present and no real future for which one could hope in human and Christian terms.

Only those are interested in a transformation of the present who do not have a share in the benefits of contemporary society or at least do not share justly therein, but are discriminated against or are being oppressed. Another and *new* future for which men hope is always aimed at the negativity of the present, concretely for those who are oppressed. The oppressors are inhuman. But the oppressed alone, who have been stripped of their humanity, really know inhumanity as objects of exploitation or racial hatred. Thus one has to listen to *them* and one has to let them talk, if one wants to get to know the real conditions of the present and wants to understand that future for which its pays to hope. A future which can be related to the ultimate good, that is, to the Godhead of God, must begin with the overcoming of the oppression of the present. The process of the transformation of thought and the change of the inhuman conditions must reach both the oppressed and the oppressors and the Christian theologians living among them. But it will grasp the oppressors and the theologians only if they no longer listen to themselves and their ilk, but to those who feel oppressed and who demand their rights.

For in listening to the oppressed, the oppressors and the theologians among them might become sensitive to the "oppression of God," the oppression God suffers in Jesus Christ and by which he liberates mankind.

(3) The central question in Teilhard, Whitehead, Bloch, and any Christian theology is evil—political and moral, physical and meta-

physical evil. What do they and we answer? Can we integrate evil
into creation as part of a world in evolution or process? Should we
better forsake the world together with evil as "just a bagatelle"? Is
evil in God himself, or is God himself suffering under the evil because his being is love? Our reason is not only scientific reason, but
is preceded by suffering and is *co-suffering reason* asking for meaning in order to live or to survive. I am not so much interested in
Teilhard in regard to what he has to say about evolution and point
Omega, which integrates everything in increasingly holistic units in
a progress of attraction, but I do take note of his view of the *garbage
can* of the kinks in the evolution of nature. Per chance it will happen
that mankind too will be dumped into this can. Our white capitalist
evolution has already dumped millions of men into it; I personally
regard Teilhard's occasional comment that this is the price to be
paid for successful evolution as sheer mockery. Together with
Dostoyevsky's Ivan Karamazov I can only say: I refuse to pay the
price. For the sake of one starving child I reject, I reject this idea of
evolution and especially its religious theodicy. My co-suffering reason is dissatisfied with a God who doesn't mind making such mis-
takes. Can the mover of this kind of evolution be called God? Why
not the devil?

I am not so much interested in Whitehead in regard to his process-
thought and his "becoming God" with a primordial and consequent
nature, though I like his phrase about God as "the great companion
—the fellow-sufferer who understands." My co-suffering reason
would wish to know what is going on in his divinity in relationship
to those abandoned, starved, bereft of their own name and their
honor, and what practical consequences follow for the philosopher
and theologian. Electromagnetic fields do not interest me relative
to a *religious Weltanschauung* congenial to my scientific reason, but
relative to the electrification of the shacks of the sharecroppers in
North Carolina and the slums of Nairobi, to mention two examples
only; and I would like to know how they correspond to my co-suffering reason. Of course, we say $2 \times 2 = 4$. But for some two days
of work times two days of work easily equals eighty dollars; for

others it equals only eight dollars. Practically $2 \times 2 = 4$ is something different in East Harlem than in Wall Street, and in Botswana something different than in Tübingen.

In regard to theology as history I can understand that Jesus in virtue of his resurrection from the dead is the real *prolepsis* or, as I would say, the incarnated promise of the coming God and thus the meaningful unity of universal history. But then in the context of the Passion Story of this world, I want to know why God raised one, rejected by his people, crucified by the ruling Romans, forsaken by his own God and Father, and made him the future of man. Not the great historical acts of God as such interest me, but the suffering of God in the Passion Story of the world. In remembering the crucified one and in facing the hopelessly suffering, we need to ponder a *revision* of future-thinking and hope-language.

(4) A future which does not begin in the transformation of the present is for me no genuine future. A hope which is not the hope of the oppressed today is no hope for which I could give a theological account. A resurrection symbol which is not the symbolizing resurrection of the crucified one does not touch me. If the theologians and philosophers of the future do not plant their feet on the ground and turn to a theology of the cross and the dialectic of the negative, they will disappear in a cloud of liberal optimism and appear a mockery of the present misery of the suffering. If we cannot justify the theme of the conference, "Hope and the Future of Man," before the present reality of the frustration and oppression of man, we are batting the breeze and talking merely for our own self-satisfaction.

Future and Unity

WOLFHART PANNENBERG

I.

Concerning the future, as with other subject matter, there exists no pre-established agreement on terms, no accepted language. Diverse judgments on particular items are intricately connected with different uses of language. This is true among theologians, as well as in the wider context of intellectual discourse. Sometimes one suspects that it is even more true among theologians so that at least this point confirms the distinctive dignity of theology. The lack of an accepted language is not necessarily disastrous, however. It favors the emergence of fresh points of view which otherwise might have been precluded from discussion. It further calls for an effort toward deeper penetration into the subject and thus gives occasion to approach a more substantial agreement. On the other hand, significant disagreement itself presupposes a common point of reference, if only as a point of departure into different directions.

In this way, I think, there is a common point of reference for theological talk about the future as compared to secular futurology. Theological language seems to be characterized by a particular emphasis on the novelty of the future. This element of novelty appears to be central in otherwise very different theological conceptions. It is given its ultimate form in eschatology. The emphasis on the novelty of existence as well as on the otherness of God and his revelation point back to Christian eschatology and to the rediscovery of eschatology since the beginning of this century. Thus eschatology seems to recommend itself as a common point of reference in the midst of theological disagreements in dealing with the future.

In some way, of course, the element of novelty is important for all talk about the future. But in the predominant perspective of secular futurologists, the future is anticipated by extrapolating the trends of what is going on at present or by developing models which are designed to meet those trends. In theology, however, the future is taken to confront and even to run counter to the present world, including the trends of its development. It is true that this way of looking at the future is particularly characteristic of the so-called theology of hope and of other European conceptions which have been developed on the basis of the exegetical rediscovery of early Christian eschatology. It is less true of the work of Teilhard de Chardin, although Teilhard also insists upon the priority of Omega over against the evolutionary process. And the idea of a future confronting and not just prolonging the present may be still less characteristic of the Whiteheadian line of thought. But even there the notion of a God providing every new occasion with its particular subjective aim allows for an appropriation of the Christian evaluation of the present in terms of its eschatological future at least to the same degree as in Bultmann's conception of the futuricity of Christian existence.

For Christian theology, the idea of God is closely connected with novelty and contingency and thus with the future. This comes to the fore in the doctrine of incarnation, as well as in the concepts of promise and of hope encouraged by promise. But the future of God which is announced by promise does not simply oppose the existing structures of the world. One reason for this lies in the very idea of promise, because promise means a positive relation of the announced future to present reality. In contrast to the threat of judgment and destruction, promise relates itself to an important interest in the existential situation of those to whom the promise is given. This concurs with the basic thrust of the idea of divine love, which affirms the present reality of the creature although it may aim at changing it into a closer image of its true destiny. Finally, this positive attitude toward present and even past reality is definitely affirmed by the Christian belief in the incarnation of God in Jesus Christ. Faith in the incarnation means that the future will not just destroy present and past. The future of God will be in many ways an extrapolation of the message and history of Jesus of Nazareth, as much as this was based on the future of the kingdom invading the present. Even the idea of judgment does not express a clash with the superior force imposing itself from the outside, but the final consequence of the intrinsic nature of the kind of behavior that is to undergo judgment. Therefore the divine judgment could be said to consist precisely in leaving men to the desires of their hearts. Thus, futurological extrapolation of contemporary trends and theological confrontation of the present by the future of God need not simply oppose each other. Especially the models designed by futurology in order to cope with the foreseeable results of tendencies observed at present can correspond significantly to theological anticipations of the future of man and the world in terms of promise and hope. The most basic difference seems to be that extrapolation is safest when it deals with the immediate or short-range future, while theology is primarily concerned with the ultimate destiny of man and of the world. But because of the increasing acceleration of change, futurology tries to anticipate also the more distant future which the theologian might call a middle-range future, while theology, on the other hand, applies its ultimate future to the present state of affairs in order to enlighten the imagination to invent solutions for the needs of the present and the more immediate future.

II.

The theological assumption that the future is not simply an extrapolation and prolongation of present and past, but a reality in its own right is based on the idea of God. Even if God is not conceived in terms of the power of the future itself, but in a more traditional way as eternal being, he is thought to create new creatures continuously, thus confronting each present with a future different from itself. And even in a more traditional view which takes God without reservation as contemporary with finite beings at present, God is not only the creator, but is himself also the future of man and of the world; for all creation is destined to participate in his glory and to be itself glorified by that eschatological participation in the glory of God.

The idea of God as future of the world, while illustrating most emphatically the theological understanding of a future confronting the present, forms at the same time a point of contact with the extrapolated future of futurology; and I shall confine my further reflections to this particular phenomenon: the God who is confronting the present world with its future and who is himself the ultimate future of man, is one and only one God. If the one God is the ultimate future of man, then the future evolution of man will tend toward a unity of mankind. Thus, the guiding principle of Teilhard de Chardin—the idea of creative unification—presents itself as a necessary implication of the idea of the one God as soon as that one God is considered not only the origin of his creation, but also its ultimate destiny and consummation, provided that his creative activity is not separated from, but related to, his future, which is to bring about through the purgatory of his judgment the reconciliation and unification of all creatures. In this point Teilhard's view seems very close to the early Christian expectation of the future kingdom of God and especially to an interpretation which becomes aware of the very reality of the creator as being tied up with the coming of his kingdom.

The dynamics of reconciliation are not something secondary to the creative activity of God, but unconditional, creative, and reconciling love characterizes the activity of the creator himself, and the evolutionary process is drawn deeper and deeper into the center of this creative dynamic notwithstanding the tendencies toward self-seclusion, self-preservation, acedia, and aggression among his creatures. Thus the process of reconciliation overcoming the horrors of human history is in some sense closer to the heart of God than former stages of the evolutionary process of life are, but it is the heart of the power that created all things which the Christian faith in reconciliation is concerned with.

While this perspective is to a considerable degree common to Teilhard and to the theologies which gravitate toward an eschatological future, the question is more difficult whether there is also a correspondence with the process thought of the Whiteheadian school. To be sure, also in Whitehead's perspective God is the source of unity by providing the subjective aim for every occasion which realizes itself by a process of subjective unification of its world. Could not this unifying activity be interpreted to mean a degree of participation in God's act of creation in the sense of Teilhard's creative unification? The difficulty is that creativity in Whitehead's own thought is separated from his idea of God. The consequence seems to be not only that Whitehead's God is hardly conceivable as creator of the world in the strict sense of a *creatio ex nihilo,* but also—and even more important—that an unlimited pluralism of events results, each of which forms a unity in itself but does not converge with all others toward a final unity of all actual occasions. It may be possible, as John Cobb proposes, to develop Whitehead's idea of God in this important respect by subordinating creativity to God as supreme entity, although this seems to require further revisions of Whitehead's conceptual framework, since God has to be concevied then as the origin of contingent existence and not merely as providing a formal ideal for each new occasion. But be this as it may, if creativity is subordinated to God's creative activity, the Teilhardian idea of a convergence of the evolutionary process toward a final unity by participation in the one God need not remain any longer excluded from the perspective of process theology. To the contrary, if love is considered to represent the ultimate motivation of God's creative activity, and if it belongs to love that the one who loves communicates himself to the beloved one to the degree that is beneficial for the beloved one, then the consummation of the process of evolution in a convergent unity by participation in the unity of the creator seems intimately connected with the act of creation as such. This does not constitute a claim of the creatures on God, but it lies in the intrinsic logic of the creative love of God himself.

III.

The prospect of a united human race emerges as an area of intersection and coincidence of the divine reality on one hand and of the extrapolated tendencies of human history and even of the entire evolution of organic life on the other.

In the Christian tradition the idea of an intersection of divine and human reality was considered the privilege of the person of Christ. And indeed, he was not only the prophet of the coming kingdom, but he also became its messiah and the pioneer and head of a new humanity. However, his messianic role does not allow keeping that privilege for himself, but consists in communicating participation in God's kingdom to others. This means pioneering justice and peace among all human beings. The kingdom of God which Jesus proclaimed to come and which by his proclamation already invaded the present of his audience is God's own ultimate reality and brings with it the reconciliation of all men in a society of peace and justice which the Old Testament prophets announced in contrast to the social and political realities of their own times. Only that future can substantiate faith in a loving God when his love will attain satisfaction in reconciling all suffering and aberration of his creatures.

Obviously this idea of the kingdom of God by far exceeds everything that could be achieved by human efforts. Or, if it is not obvious, it will become more evident in the course of this discussion. And yet that idea provides an appropriate criterion for measuring the degree of achievement in social and political efforts and changes. There is a correspondence between the future of God's kingdom and the apparently blind forces working in the process of human history, in spite of the deficiencies and perversions of history. Even the social and political urge toward the unity of men is marked by deep ambiguities. And yet its correspondence with the unity of God's kingdom that is to come testifies to the fact that human history in the midst of its perversions continues to be the creation of the God whose kingdom is coming.

For Teilhard de Chardin the phenomenon of a convergent drift in the evolution of the human race and especially in the modern phase of human history was of utmost importance. While the evolution of life generally displays a divergent tendency in the formation of an abundant multitude of species and of immense numbers of individuals, on the level of the human race a tendency to the contrary develops—a drift toward unity. The decisive condition for this turn of the evolutionary process is, in Teilhard's view, the human capability for reflection. Unfortunately, Teilhard did not elaborate to a great extent on his concept of human reflection. But this much is clear, that reflection is related, in his view, to the ability of man to form universal ideas, and this makes possible the convergent process of the association of individuals in the history of mankind. The suggestion that man is the social animal precisely because he is the reflective animal is open to considerable refinement. And it is a crucial point, because the interrelation of individual and society lies at the very heart of all human problems and especially of the problems concerning the future of man. One could complement Teilhard's rare remarks by the observation that man's capacity for the universal is related to the fact that man does not possess the unity of his existence within himself and therefore is constantly looking for a unity beyond himself but comprising him. George Herbert Mead's statement that the identity of the individual is a social fact provides a corollary of this. Because man has no definitive unity in himself, the social unit is constitutive for the identity of the human individual, although it is transcended in its turn by his quest for the universal.

On the basis of the reflective character of human existence, the continuous population increase gains its specific significance for the evolution of the human race. It develops together with the spread of the human race all over the earth. This global expansion, of course, takes the form of the economic and political expansion of concrete social units, and their expansion leads to collisions and warfare. All this entered a period of acceleration toward a critical climax in modern times because of the development of science and technology. Teilhard was presumably right in assuming that the result has been an increasing pressure toward socialization on a global level. The population increase due to modern medical technology and to intensified communications and trade as a consequence of the industrial revolution represented only an initial phase. With the development of nuclear weapons military technology reached a degree which amounts to a compulsion to peace, at least among the great powers. It has been argued that this involves, in the long run, a pressure toward some sort of world government. In any event, there is good reason for the assertion of Alvin Toffler that today already "the network of social ties is so tightly woven that the consequences of contemporary events radiate instantaneously around the world."[1] The repercussions of the Vietnam war illustrate this statement.

IV.

Teilhard de Chardin was rather confident concerning the convergent trend in the recent history of man. He certainly recognized some of the negative aspects connected with the increasing demographic compression. He saw the increasing density of population leading to intensified aggression, to extreme nervousness, and to the spread of neurosis. However, in his view these problems are only temporary. The increasing compression will necessitate a new level of association and organization of the individuals, and thus the tension will be relieved. While this may be a possible development of the present historical situation, it is by no means certain, and its intrinsic dangers must not be overlooked. Teilhard himself recognized the possibility of a perversion of the modern principle of convergent totalization—the manipulation and standardization of the human masses, the termitary of collectivism instead of the fraternization of men. But he regarded these alarming tendencies as only temporary deviations from the course of evolution. He underestimated the abyss of alienation in the trend toward the megamachine society.

On the one hand it is certainly true that there will be no future for man outside his association with all other men. There is a considerable degree of truth in Teilhard's judgment about the heresy of individualism. His judgment does not only hit the tendency to self-isolation in traditional bourgeois individualism. It is particularly pertinent with regard to romantic reactions against the megamachine society, reactions that like to stylize themselves as radical or revolutionary but in reality only give voice to a powerless protest against the restrictive impact of modern society on individual life by insisting on the right to develop all natural talents and to follow all individual desires. Tendencies of this kind in the subcultures as well as in the psychological and educational thought may be colorful and at least sometimes deserve our sympathy. But they are romantic in character, because the increasing density of population as well as the multiplication of possible choices will enforce a higher degree of mutual respect and considerateness among people, rather than allow more room for arbitrariness even in the sanctuaries of privacy which will continue to compensate for the hardships of social life.

There is enormous pressure toward increasing unification in social life as is the case in world politics. But on the other hand, the tension between individual and society will continue. The common interest needs to be articulated and put into action by individuals. Therefore, again and again the common cause will be exploited by individuals for their own purposes and self-interests. The anonymous structures of social organization serve only to disguise the domination of men by other men. This is not only true of the capitalist economy in the Western world; it also applies to the power structures in non-capitalist countries. The exploitation of the common cause by individuals is so deeply rooted in the present condition of human existence that it will prevent, in the foreseeable future, any definitive conquest of alienation. If this factor is not taken into account, ideological delusions become inevitable.

It is precisely this observation that reascertains the principle that the individual must remain the purpose of the social system. This principle can easily be misused or mistaken as a full license for arbitrary individualism. In fact it is primarily a measure to prevent the abuse of political or economic power. But underlying it is a recognition of the fact that any imaginable improvement of the human condition must improve the situation of the individual, because, after all, mankind exists only in the form of individual human beings. Certainly the destiny of the individual himself is beyond himself. But the unity beyond himself which enables his reflective existence is attainable only through the inspiration of personal freedom. Therefore not the arbitrary individual, but the free person must remain the standard for judging the social organization. But what marks the difference between responsible personality which ought to be respected and encouraged and an arbitrary individualism that must be limited wherever it injures the social or natural living conditions of other people? In final analysis this will turn out to be a religious question, because the distinction between responsible freedom and arbitrariness touches on the most fundamental issues concerning the destiny of man.

V.

The ambiguities in the convergence toward unity which characterize the present period of human history have become apparent. They reside in the tensions between the individual and social destiny of man. On the one hand, the individual does not possess the meaning of his existence in himself. In order to establish himself, he needs a unity beyond himself, and this is concretely at hand in the group or society to which the individual belongs. On the other hand, the purpose of the society itself should be the individual, because otherwise there will be suppression of individuals in the name of the common interest of the society or even of mankind which happens, however, to be represented by other individuals and their judgments. This is the intricate situation that apparently does not allow any simple way out of alienation: there is the alienation of an official consciousness, which denies the individual his free judgment, and there is the opposite alienation of arbitrary individualism, which denies the individual the consciousness of a unity of truth beyond his arbitrary choices and still makes him feel dominated by others who take advantage of his basic human needs.

Obviously, a definitive solution for the antagonism of individual and society remains an eschatological ideal. It is not likely to be attained under the present conditions of human history. The problem could be solved if men were good by nature expecting their satisfaction only from the common good and not using the common good as means for their self-interest. But men are not good in this sense, and therefore the antagonisms between the individual and society as among the individuals themselves will not be definitively overcome under the present or similar conditions of existence. The definitive removal of all alienation would require the accomplishment of the human destiny of the individual as well as of the society, and it would require that all human individuals should be granted a share in that perfect society. That is the meaning precisely of the Jewish and Christian eschatological imagery which is expressed by combining the kingdom of God and the resurrection of the dead: the expectation of the kingdom of God implies that only when God rules and no man possesses dominating political power any more, then the domination of people by other people and the injustice inevitably connected with it will come to an end. The alternative to the rule of men over other men is not actually self-government, because those who govern or take part in an administration are always a small minority. The true alternative is the rule of God. That alone will replace human rule and bring about a society without a rule of men over men, thus accomplishing the social destiny of man. The second condition is the participation of all individuals according to their capacity to participate. This is not to be achieved except in the presence of all human individuals. It takes a resurrection of the dead to have all human individuals of all times participate in the perfect society of the kingdom of God. Only on this condition the destiny of mankind which comprises the total number of its individuals can be claimed to be accomplished. If the social and individual destinies of man condition each other so that they can be realized only together, then the totality of human individuals is required for the realization of the social destiny of man. It is not enough to hope for a perfect society in a more or less distant future and for a later generation. That would only mean to sacrifice the present generation for the pretended welfare of a future one—a dedication that is usually expected without asking the victim for his consent. On the contrary, the symbolism of the Jewish-Christian eschatological expectation spells out very precisely the conditions for a definitive accomplishment of the human destiny in a truly human society.

VI.

What kind of future does the eschatological symbolism of the Jewish-Christian tradition refer to? There is no doubt that it was understood as actual future in the sense that it is not yet but is still to come. Moreover it was often understood as an event in line with all other events. But here the questions arise. A general resurrection of the dead would obviously be an event which as an event would be out of comparison with any other event. How then can it be imagined to be a member of the same sequence with events of the ordinary kind? If in some way a general resurrection of the dead is to follow other events, then also the temporal sequence itself might be of a different kind than sequences the members of which are all ordinary events. One might think of a deformation of the ordinary form of temporal sequence comparable to the contortion of space according to the theory of relativity.

The suspicions concerning the sequence from ordinary historical events to those events which the eschatological symbolism of the Christian tradition refers to increase when one reads in the Jewish apocalyptic writings that the events that are to be revealed in the end-time already pre-exist in heaven. This pattern of thought can also be found in the New Testament, especially in the Gospel of John, where it indicates that the future judgment happens already now in the confrontation with Jesus Christ and that those who believe his words participate even now in eternal life. Similarly the epistle to the Collossians says that the baptized Christians are not only united with the death of Christ and given the hope of future resurrection, as Paul had argued, but that they already now participate also in the new life of the resurrection, although it is still hidden with God. And is it not strikingly similar to this way of reasoning when Christ is said to rule already now in the mysterious secrecy of God, in heaven, over the powers that dominate the world? The messianic kingdom of the future is already present in heaven. And thus in a secret way Jesus already was the messiah and the Son of Man when he walked on earth. All this means that the eschatological future in some way is already present, although in secrecy and mystery which is the essence of heaven apart from the spatial image of a divine region up there beyond the stars. The same holds true even of God himself: his kingdom and thus the public execution of his power being a matter of the eschatological future, God is already ruling the world from the hiddenness of heaven.

The eschatological future is identical with the eternal essence of things, just as the future of God's kingdom is his eternal life and power. Is it, therefore, no longer a true future? Well, it is, because the essence of things did not yet break the surface. It has not yet been brought forth. And yet it is the essence of things past and present. Hence in some way it must be itself past or present. We have to revise the traditional understanding of essence and eternity regarding their relation to time. The essence of things is not to be conceived as something non-temporal; but it depends on the temporal process and will be decided upon only by its outcome, although it may be the identity of things long past. Correspondingly, eternity—being the realm of essential truth—is not to be conceived as non-temporal, but constituted by the historical process and especially by its final outcome. On the other hand, time is not just a sequence of momentary events, but of events that contribute to the identity or essence of things. While Teilhard did not bother himself with such questions, I know that statements like these must sound strange to Whiteheadians. However, I cannot help but recognize a series of strictly momentary events as an abstract quantification of actual processes, and such a quantification—remarkably enough—has to be complemented by a Platonic realm of mere possibilities. But in every process there develops something, and that something is not merely an aggregate of momentary events, nor is it just a possibility; it is developing and enduring not only as an object, but also in itself. This is nothing else than what has been called the substance or essence of things. I agree with process philosophy that the traditional idea of substance was wrong because it was falsely separated from temporal existence and development. But I am not convinced that it is even possible to completely abolish the notion of essence. If we take being and time, essence and temporal existence together, then we get involved in the paradoxes of present and future as they were mentioned earlier. Then a final future is going to decide definitively about the essence of things. This future, then, will not be merely accidental to the substance of the thing which it will determine. On the other hand, it will not be simply identical with the essence it determines. This brings us back to the question of what kind of future the eschatological hope is looking for. Now the answer can be given: it is the essential future of mankind, the accomplishment of the destiny of man. In other words, it is an anticipation of the impact of unknown future events on the essence of man—on each individual as on the human race. It is as much an anticipation as every statement which identifies the nature of a phenomenon, except for its explicit distinction between the present situation of man and his future destiny. And as every anticipation does, it leaves the question open as to the particular events which will bring about the anticipated future.

The syndrome of future and eternity, which in Jewish-Christian eschatology allows for an anticipation of definitive truth, is of particular importance for the self-understanding of man. The hope of man is never progress, at least not just progress, but the important question is where the progress is progressing to. Man hopes for achievement and for an achievement not to be lost again. Human hope yearns for eternity, and this provides the standard for true progress that is not just continuous and empty change. The fascination of progress depends on the degree to which it reflects eternity. It not only approaches achievement, but already participates in it because the essential future penetrates into the present. The essential future participates in eternity and therefore constitutes the depth of reality, the mystery of the present. Only because the essential future is already present can it be anticipated, and thus provide identity to our personal life even now, although the process of our lives is still open. A future without eternity amounts to meaningless change; and if people get exposed to that kind of essentially empty future, future shock results, because meaningless change endangers our personal identity. The continuous rise of transience, novelty, and diversity in the social environment of men in the present and in the foreseeable future which Alvin Toffler so aptly described, will seriously aggravate the dangers of future shock and will render it more and more difficult to achieve personal identity. On the other hand, only a strong personal identity can endure the rise of transience, novelty, and diversity in our social world. I agree with Erich Fromm that mere adaptation is not enough; it deprives man of his human dignity by turning him into an alienated, though possibly useful, element of the megamachine society. In order to preserve the human character of private and of public life, personal identity is indispensable. But identity is possible only by anticipation of the eternal. This is implied when Erich Fromm calls for "centers of orientation and devotion" as belonging to the very conditions of human existence.[2] They provide the individual with a frame of orientation about himself and about his rapidly changing world and direct his devotion to what constitutes his human destiny. In the midst of increasing transience, novelty, and diversity such centers of orientation and devotion are all the more needed for constituting zones of stability in the process of our lives where we can resist future shock.

VII.

To articulate the human need for centers of orientation and devotion means to raise the question of religion. The individual does not find his personal identity by adaptation to the secular standards of society, for society is composed of men fallible like himself. In former periods of history when society was understood as imaging the eternal order of things, it was easier to take its standards for the eternal truth itself than it is in a period of rapid and still increasing social change. But even in those early historical periods, society on its own part was in need of a religious foundation. Only the assumption that the principles and symbolic institutions of a society represent the final truth of all reality—only that assumption can secure the loyalty of the individual for his social order as Eric Voegelin has explained. Thus the antagonism between individual and social order was solved in history again and again by religion. Even the prevailing contemporary models of social order have in this sense a religious foundation. The socialist societies are based on the assumption that they incorporate the final truth of human destiny for this period of history. And the political principles of Western democracy similarly are assumed to be basic conditions of human dignity. However the principles of the freedom and equality of men are neither self-evident, nor do they in fact determine the actual structures of social life in the societies of the Western world. They are not self-evident, for strictly speaking the majority of individuals are empirically neither free nor equal, except to different degrees. That the two principles do not determine the actual structure of social life was Karl Marx' criticism of Western democracy: in the bourgeois democracy there exists only a formal equality and a formal freedom veiling the actual inequality of the conditions and means to make use of that freedom. One may argue that such a formal freedom is still better than none at all, and this, of course, accounts for the superiority of liberal democracy until the present time. But it is not a very strong justification and offers but little confidence in view of the possibilities of a liberalization in socialist societies which could definitively steal away the focus of political imagination from Western democracy.

The most serious weakness of the democratic societies of the West continues to be, as an increasing number of observers agree, that the unity of society is primarily based on economic interest forming the common denominator for all individuals in the processes of production and consumption. Almost everything else is reduced to a private concern and thus again left to the market that mediates between production and consumption of the goods of culture as of other objects for private desires. The religion of privacy is just the reverse side of the economic-centered character of our society.

But the concern for the meaning of human life that unites the individual to the rest of mankind is not reducible to economic interest nor to private preference. This explains the uneasiness which has befallen so many sensitive members of the Western countries and also the unexpected extent of fascination by the quasi-religious character of the socialist societies.

My personal conclusion is that the Western societies desperately need a reappropriation and revision of their religious heritage which once provided the religious foundations of their beginnings. Since the problem of social unity is finally a religious one, because religion articulates the awareness of the future destiny of man that bridges over the antagonism between individual and society, therefore religion cannot remain, in the long run, an exclusively private concern. The privatization of religion in modern times was a necessary measure against the dogmatic intolerance that resulted in the confessional wars at the beginning of modern times. Religious intolerance disrupted the social peace. Therefore, the Christian religion could no longer provide the basis for a unified society, and the Christian religion can never again represent the spiritual unity of a society if it does not overcome the confessional conflicts of the past. But Christianity cannot solve the problems of its own antagonistic traditions without facing the general problem of a pluralism of religious thought due to the provisional status of all religious experience and knowledge in contrast to the final truth about God and man that is still to come, although it has been anticipated in Jesus Christ. Such a reflection on the preliminary character of religious knowledge may not only reconcile the conflicting confessional traditions in Christianity, but also opens up the Christian consciousness for the truth of other religious traditions and perspectives. On the other hand, such a legitimation of the pluralism of religious experience and thought within the Christian tradition and even beyond its limits represents, by itself, a new type of unified religious thought. It seems to be this type of religious thought that will become increasingly important for the future of the society and for an emerging unity of mankind, if the society will not regress to a more authoritarian and intolerant form of religious or quasi-religious foundation. In order to prevent this and to strengthen the more pluralistic possibilities of religious thought and piety without surrendering, however, the unity of truth, it is important to become aware of the fact that the new form of religious thought that emerges today from innumerable ecumenical encounters and dialogues is no longer merely a private conviction.

There is much disenchantment with the ecumenical movement today, and there are many reasons for that. But one should not overlook that the ecumenical movement might very well turn out to represent the most far-reaching contribution of Christianity to the political future of humanity and particularly to that of the Western world. This conjecture does not refer primarily to the declarations of the ecumenical council of churches on specific problems of social and political life. It would be a mistake to seek the significance of ecumenical activities predominantly in that field. The relevance of comments on social and political problems from ecumenical organizations and officials depends finally on their religious competence. And it is the theological dialogue, the religious reconciliation that will have the most revolutionary social and political consequences, because the religious problem lies at the very root of social and political unity. Therefore, whoever is concerned for the long-range aspects of the political responsibilities of the Christian faith should devote his efforts to the ecumenical cause, if he is not already induced to do so by other reasons. The ecumenical dialogue is the process where today the eschatological destiny and future of man and the approach of mankind toward increasing unity must obviously coincide.

NOTES

[1]Alvin Toffler, *Future Shock* (New York: Random House, 1970), p. 17.

[2]Erich Fromm, *The Revolution of Hope: Toward a Humanized Technology* (New York: Harper & Row, 1968), p. 62.

Response to
Wolfhart Pannenberg

DONALD P. GRAY

In a course of lectures delivered in the early 1960's on the history of Protestant theology during the last two centuries, Paul Tillich took as his guiding thematic "the continuous series of attempts to unify the diverging elements of the modern mind." He spoke of the most important of these attempts as seeking "to unite the orthodox and the humanist traditions." "All modern theology," he argued, "is an attempt to unite these two trends in the recent history of Christian thought." Looking back over the nineteenth and early twentieth centuries, Tillich pictured the whole story of modern theology in dramatic terms. He maintained that "it is the drama of the rise of a humanism in the midst of Christianity which is critical of the Christian tradition, departs from it and produces a vast world of secular existence and thought. Then there is the rise of some of the greatest philosophers and theologians who try to unite these divergent elements again. Their syntheses in turn are destroyed and the divergent elements collide and try to conquer each other, and new attempts to reunite them have to be made."[1]

Evolutionary theologies of process, both in their Whiteheadian and Teilhardian forms, as well as the eschatological theologies of hope, represent just such attempts to go beyond humanism at the same time that they seek to reunite "the diverging elements of the modern mind." They may all be viewed as efforts toward a viable and responsible form of Christian humanism in contemporary society, a Christian humanism which seeks. to be faithful to the great themes of biblical and classical Christianity as well as to the humanist concern for man and his future. Each seeks to meet the critical accusations of humanism against Christian faith by reinterpreting the Christian tradition in the light of these accusations. This dialogue with humanism, it seems to me, constitutes a very basic and decisive bond of unity among those theological perspectives, a bond of unity which should not be lost sight of in our discussions. To some extent, in fact, we can say that the very differences between these points of view derive from the differing traditions of humanism which serve as dialogue partners in each case; on the one hand, the traditions of scientific and evolutionary humanism and, on the other, the traditions of Marxist and revolutionary humanism.

In one sense, a conference on hope and the future of man which does not include humanism is incomplete. In another sense a conference which does include these three theologies of the future must inevitably come to grips with the humanistic questioning to which these theologies are in large measure a response. Humanism is a tradition of hope in the modern world and it often expresses this hope in the terms which Professor Pannenberg has chosen to make central to his presentation: the unity of mankind. In this common concern for a not-yet-existing community of fellowship, Christian and secular humanism find a meeting place for discussion and joint action. And yet a certain opposition between the two with regard to the importance to be assigned to belief in God and immortality in the quest for unity remains apparently intractable.

This opposition is brought to a rather concise crystallization by the English humanist H. J. Blackham: "Humanism proceeds from an assumption *that* man is on his own and this life is all and an assumption *of* responsibility for one's own life and for the life of mankind."[2] While each of these three theologies affirms the necessity of personal and social responsibility, each likewise rejects the assumption that man is on his own. By way of countering this critical assertion each of these theologies has sought to reconstruct traditional understandings of God in the direction of a new definition of both the place and nature of God's presence and activity in human history. Important differences of approach to the question of God do indeed exist among these theologies and require further exploration in relation to humanistic objections.

When we come to consider the place of life beyond death in relation to Blackham's humanist claim that this life is all, we discover a somewhat more complicated situation which I should like to dwell on briefly because of its importance in Professor Pannenberg's talk. Humanists have objected to belief in life beyond death for a variety of reasons. For some there simply exists no cogent evidence for it. For others it violates the contemporary anthropological perception of the psychosomatic unity of man. For still others it is ethically repellent in that it seems to foster a self-centered individualism of reward and punishment. It is also often rejected as leading to an irresponsible otherworldliness that neglects the momentous problems of modern social life and the human future. Theologians have generally shown themselves in recent work to be refreshingly open to these objections and have tried to meet some of them at least through an emphasis on the Christian symbol of resurrection, entailing as it does a social understanding of eschatological hope along with an expectation of the transformation of the whole of reality. This emphasis is unmistakably evident in the theological work of Professor Pannenberg and in the writings of Teilhard de Chardin as well. Process theologians, on the other hand, following Whitehead's lead, have generally stressed an objective immortality in the divine memory rather than a personal immortality. While not usually denying dogmatically the possibility of survival beyond death, they have frequently, though not unanimously, argued against its necessity and stressed its dangers. Process theologians have also been reluctant, as Professor Pannenberg notes, to assign

any definitive goal or destination to the historical process, prefer-
ring in this way to underline the consistent openendedness of the
process. There are many merits in these proposals, but they do represent a point of some conflict between the respective theological
positions.

The question which the eschatological theology of Professor
Pannenberg and the evolutionary theology of Teilhard perhaps
pose to a Whiteheadian perspective and beyond it to contemporary
humanism has to do with the issue of meaning as it is affected by
our convictions regarding life after death. Because of the widespread crisis of traditions so evident throughout the modern world,
a deep and abiding problem of meaninglessness has appeared in
Western culture particularly, a problem which gravely threatens
man's commitment to carry the historical movement forward to
unification. Rejection of the eschatological symbols of personal resurrection and cosmic transformation at least runs the risk of enforc-
ing this sense of ultimate meainglessness. A belief which at one
moment in human history seemed to undermine man's concern for
the human future is seen by some today as possessing considerable
potency for building the earth. If one replies that man lives on in
the historical process as such through his labors or even in the
divine memory, does this not unduly weight the social side of existence against the personal? Is there not a danger in this context that
man's function in the process will be of considerably larger importance than man himself? Does not the biblical symbol of the kingdom of God which comprehends all things together in a union
which is also differentiating or personalizing (as Teilhard
remarks), more adequately resolve the tension between the social
and the personal, a tension whose importance today Professor Pannenberg so rightly stresses?

The broad agreement I feel with Professor Pannenberg's paper is
certainly not unconnected with the evident sympathy he expresses
for Teilhard's vision. Lest I appear to be wholly in agreement with
him, however, I should like to address a question to his paper from
a Teilhardian vantage point. For Teilhard the unification of all

things which is the end is prepared for in the historical process through the earth-building activities of men. In a real sense, the end is conditioned by men's work. In this way Teilhard seeks to overcome the humanistic charge of otherworldliness by refusing the Christian the privilege of leaping over history so as to get to the end prematurely. The way to the end is through history and the world. Clearly for Professor Pannenberg, the end as man's unity promised by God is intended to lead to a socially serious ethic of historical responsibility. But what is the precise nature of the dialectic between what God promises now and gives in the end and man's response in hope-filled activity or his failure of response in hopeless inactivity?

I have tried in this reaction to point up the shared relationship between these differing theological styles and the humanist critique of the Christian tradition in modern times. I have focused my attention primarily on the humanist rejection of Christian eschatology and the varying responses to this in these three theologies of the future. I have tried to see lines of convergence as well as lines of divergence. In conclusion, I should like simply to say that as a Teilhardian I have learned a great deal from Professor Pannenberg and can only welcome with appreciation his sympathetic reading of and interest in Teilhard de Chardin.

NOTES

[1] Paul Tillich, *Perspectives in 19th and 20th Century Protestant Theology,* ed. Carl E. Braaten (New York: Harper & Row, 1967), pp. 4-5.

[2] H. J. Blackham, *Humanism* (Baltimore: Penguin Books, 1968), p. 13.

Response to
Wolfhart Pannenberg

DANIEL DAY WILLIAMS

Professor Pannenberg's theological work has been engaging the attention of many of us for some time, and it is a great privilege to have him in this place, to hear this wonderfully comprehensive paper, and to enter into discussion with him. I find his theological method and outlook very congenial. My questions are directed to his paper for clarification and for sharpening some issues which I believe are issues for all Christian thought, and certainly for my own.

To keep this paper brief I will confine myself to some remarks about his discussion of process theology. But I will first state where I find myself in strong agreement with him.

First, Professor Pannenberg recognizes Whitehead's doctrine of the entry of the future into every present. God's life has futurity within it for God himself embraces the realm of possibility in his being. I would only want to make even more emphatic the point that God not only holds future possibility before every actuality in the world, drawing it forward into the future; but that God in his being is Free Subject, responding to his world, making his free decisions with respect to that world, and sharing in the world's suffering and joy as he moves into his future. In Jesus Christ God has not only given us promises but has identified his life with us in love and thus created a new relationship which is the decisive content of hope and promise for all who respond to him in trust.

In the second place, Professor Pannenberg insists, quite rightly I believe, that Christian hope for the future always involves some recognition of the present love of God. There is no point in living by the promise if we have no idea of what the promise means. The kingdom is present now, though in a hidden way, and here Pannenberg does justice not only to the futurism in the New Testament but also to the theme of eternity penetrating time as it occurs in the Fourth Gospel and in many of the letters of Paul.

Third, I agree completely with his view that Christian hope does not permit us to have a purely optimistic view of the course of history. There is little evidence that the compacting of mankind leads in itself to an expanded consciousness. Go to Northern Ireland today, or any one of scores of communities within walking distance of us tonight, or let us look into our own consciences. Are we less parochial because we are more crowded in our cities? Process thought, and here I take it I am in agreement with Professor Pannenberg, holds that the question of the nature and limits of the possibilities of convergence toward a peaceful world community must be assessed empirically through historical experience. There is no inevitability about it.

Fourth, he pleads powerfully for a socialized world, a radical corrective of the individualism of Western culture. Here surely we must agree about the direction Christian action must take. I could only add that I believe theology should concern itself with the "middle range" problems of hope as well as with the ultimate and immediate problems. The life of nations, societies, communities needs the responsible criticism and direction which may come from religious thought. And surely we all hope for the ecumenical movement to have its impact on the world society, as far as we may still be from realizing full community even within the church itself.

Fifth, I accept fully Professor Pannenberg's view of the responsibility of theology to take account of the questions about what things are and how we know questions that philosophers discuss. Theology has its responsibility to appropriate philosophical insight and achieve clarity on ultimate philosophic issues.

I wish now to raise the single question which I find central to Professor Pannenberg's paper and to his discussion of process theology. It is the question of the relation of hope to the unity of God, of the world, and of truth. Let me state first what I take to be this thesis, then note his criticism of process thought on this point, and then make some suggestions as to why I hold process theology to be a viable interpretation to the Bible and of man's situation. The point has to do with the "final event" which Pannenberg asserts must unify the whole of history and disclose its meaning.

Professor Pannenberg recognizes that Christian faith is through and through eschatological. This means for him that temporality is a characteristic of all reality and of God himself. History actually contributes to the identity or essence of things. He says: "The essence of things . . . depends on the temporal process and will be decided upon only by its outcome . . . eternity is not to be conceived as non-temporal, but constituted by the historical process and especially by its final outcome" (p. 72).

Now what does Professor Pannenberg see in process thought which differs from this position? This, I think: he sees process theology as having a more loosely organized universe in which there is an endless plurality of events; and therefore no final event which consummates or determines the unity of the whole. He does not state his position in exactly this way, but this is what I understand him to say. For example, he says that Whitehead splits creativity off from God so that it can, so to speak, "go its own way" and that therefore no unity is given for the whole, and therefore hope can never be directed toward one event in which the destiny of man is accomplished.

This is why when Professor Pannenberg says that the essence of things is temporal, and that eternity is constituted by the historical process, he remarks that Whiteheadians will find this statement strange. Surely this is what Whiteheadians have argued for, that being is temporal, that history contributes to the eternal life of God. But Professor Pannenberg is right: there is something different from process thought in what he is saying. He thinks that if we are to speak hopefully of the future, we must assert a final event which constitutes the unity of the whole or else we have no decisive standard of truth and no real fulfillment of man's destiny.

Parenthetically, I may comment on one of Pannenberg's characterizations of Whiteheadian cosmology. He suggests that Whitehead's world is composed of a stream of momentary events comple-

mented by a realm of "mere possibilities" and this he sees as a
kind of Platonism. But this is not an accurate characterization of
Whitehead's view in which there are no mere possibilities. All possibilities are related to the concrete action of God and the real
events in the world. They are possibilities of value and structure
which may be exemplified in the ongoing of events. No event is
merely momentary. It grasps possibility as an element in its becoming, but it also grasps its past and the other actual entities which
become data for it. Further every event is experienced by God in
his everlasting life and power. It lives on in its function of objective
immortality for other events and for God.

I return to the Pannenberg thesis that there must be a final event
which constitutes the meaning of the whole. Two points here can
help to clear some ground.

First, Whiteheadians do not split creativity off from God. The
creativity is nothing by itself. It is simply a name for the fact that
all things participate in a dynamic interaction. But this does mean
that the notion of a "final event" becomes a contradiction for this
metaphysical view because God's creative action does not end.

Second, Pannenberg believes that Whiteheadians deny an essence for the whole of things. There is some terminological difficulty
here because Pannenberg uses essence for reality itself. The essence
of things as he sees it is the whole concrete process from beginning
to end including the final event which constitutes the identity or at
least the manifestation of the identity in the whole. Now Whiteheadians do not deny the concept of essence. For them the essence
of anything is an abstract structure which characterizes it. God has
an essence. It is the formal structure of his being which includes
the structures of possibility. This essence has identity. It does not
change. It is not modified. But God's concrete temporal life is more
than his essence. It is the reality of his creative responsible action,
moving in communion, judgment and redemption in relation to his
world. What Whiteheadians do say is that the unity of the creative
process is to be found in the community of God's being with his
creatures, not in absolute unity which is summed up in a final

event. Pannenberg is quite right in saying that process thought sees a certain inevitable plurality in being. The reason for this from the process point of view is that if God is love he must have a world to love, to act upon, and respond to. The creatures in that world must have their measure of freedom, creativity, and unique value if they are real things and not just mechanical expression of a prearranged plan.

Pannenberg does indeed say that the future will not be "simply identical" with the essence it determines (p. 73). It is in that little but mighty word "simply" that the whole issue lies. If the future is not *simply* identical with the essence, then what does it add? And if it really adds something, are we not really accepting the process view that in place of identity we have community between past and present and future.

My reasons for holding to the process view rather than accepting this single event constituting the unity of history can be stated both biblically and ethically.

As to the Scripture, the New Testament gives us at least two eschatological pictures of the end and not one. In one there is universal salvation. All things are made new. God's life embraces the whole, and all is redeemed. In the other, God divides the good from the evil in judgment. Some are lost. We should not be diverted by pathological conceptions of hell with God willing the eternal torment of his creature. The question is whether there is a real risk of lostness in being. I do not see that Professor Pannenberg's paper quite deals with this question. His final event seems to require the first option, an absolutely universal consummation which is the essence of every event, no matter what relation to good and evil it may sustain.

But I must ask, how can life be serious if in a final event it will all be one absolute good, no matter what has happened?

We can put the same point ethically in relation to the nature of love. Pannenberg speaks of the intrinsic logic of love. But surely this intrinsic logic includes the acceptance of the risk of creative freedom. Love is not the demand for the conformity of the other to an ideal; but the acceptance of the adventure of life into an unknown future. Love does not ask for guarantees. Why should love demand final completion when its very joy is participation in the task yet to be done, the anticipation of the community yet to be created? Of course there is rest, rest in every glimpse of fulfillment and every moment of communion. The intrinsic logic of love is not that of identity but that of creative community in which real suffering and loss are risked.

To open the discussion then with Professor Pannenberg where I believe we must take it, I suggest the following thesis: it is he who is the Platonist, or rather the Neo-Platonist who demands that the essence of things be identical with the transcendent One. Perhaps I misunderstand what he means by the final event which is identical with the beginning; but his view seems to be to take real hope away, for how can we hope if what things are and are becoming is really nothing more than what they have always been?

Hope and the
Biomedical Future of Man

JÜRGEN MOLTMANN

I. POETRY AND THE POLITICS OF HOPE

Our conference is intended not only theologically and philosophically to clarify the concepts *hope* and *future*, but also to develop desirable and realizable *models* of the future. Let me immediately introduce a concrete instance. There is the field of biomedical science and technology where we notice an amazing kind of progress. Here life is changed in hitherto unknown ways, involving life expectancy and the meaning of life. But, we soon ask, which changes are desirable and which are not? We must arrive at an answer today, not tomorrow, so that no irreversible processes will take place and we don't "fall backwards into the future," as Paul Valéry put it, into a future which, though we ourselves make it, we actually don't want.

Theology, within the life of a community, can perform many functions. One function would be to afford symbolic expression of the contemporary religious sensibility. In anxiety and hope, uncertainty and confidence, in suffering and happiness our sensibility and its concrete expressions always transcend the merely empirical. Theology is always involved in the "culture" of our sensibility. It also always belongs to the public poetry of the fundamental sensibility of its age. The *Theology of Hope*, too, had an historical context for its origins in the 1960's to which it owes its wide response.

Part of this context was the enthusiasm of the Kennedy era, the new "socialism with a human face" in Czechoslovakia, the "revolution of rising expectations" in the third world, Vatican II in the Roman Catholic Church, and the socio-political upsurge in the ecumenical movement. But sensibilities change very quickly. No less than five years ago everyone would have welcomed our conference theme "Hope and the Future of Man" without reservation. Today, for many of us, it sounds deceptive—too optimistic. For it seems to presuppose that mankind still has a future, and that we need only the zest of hope in order to grasp this future and find happiness. It sounds good, but in terms of old folk wisdom, it is "too good to be true." In keeping with the "culture" of our present sensibility our conference theme ought to sound a totally different note: "Frustration and the suffering of man."

In view of contemporary history, things do not look too hopeful. The hopes of the 1960's have "gone with the wind." We hear everywhere words like "frustration" and "betrayal," words that apparently are becoming keywords of our present *Lebensgefühl*.[1] Everywhere people feel deceived, abused, dispirited, exploited, and estranged so that they no longer trust the inbuilt goals and hopes of our progressive societies, universities, churches, and sciences. They refuse to live goal-oriented and future-conscious, since they refuse to freeze that future in its present image. They sense the messianic crises of those hope-movements which overshoot their mark and leave man alone in his disappointment. The theology of our present sensibility thus tends again toward apocalyptic sentiment, as expressed in the phrase from a song by Bobby Goldsboro which Hans Hoekendijk sent me in anticipation of this conference: "It's time for him to come back home, because the time is running out and the world is slowly dying. . . ."

A revision of hope theology and the future-oriented philosophies of Teilhard and Bloch would thus, in a new form, have to take note of the problems of radical evil, the absurdity of misdirected evolutionary processes, of death and the tragedy of human existence in order to arrive at an expression of solid human hope.

But theology also has another function. It is not only a religious symbolism of anxiety and hope, but also a political initiative in the conflicts of the present. It shares in and cooperates with the presence of the future in scientific progress and politico-ethical decisions.

The question of the future is a problem of the present. For only he can plan the future who already has the power to bring it about. All plans and models of the future must take into account the power constellations of the present and then extrapolate the future desired by the controlling powers. Such extrapolations, however, do not anticipate a new future, but merely extend the old present *into* the future. To determine the future on grounds of the present is always conservative. "The transposition of the present does not result in any future."[2] To the contrary, all it amounts to in fact is the imposition of present conditions on the future. A future that is to amount to more than a continuation of the present must take into account the change of the present social, political, and moral conditions. The future is different from the present only if it begins by changing the present. Interested, however, in a change of present conditions are only those who suffer from them because they have no just share in life. Hope for a new and different future is possible only among the suffering and the oppressed. Genuine future thus always focuses on the negativity of the present. And the ones who *do* hope and *can* hope for a genuinely new future are those who exist on the shadow side of the present. They do not extrapolate their hopes from the positive experience of the present, but anticipate a future which they do not have thus far. The desirable and hopeful future is anticipated in historical suffering and in suffering history, thus having its *Sitz im Leben* among the suffering. This point has to be underscored lest hope language become the ideology of the affluent among us and of the entrepreneur classes.

But one has to realize that also the hopes of the oppressed and suffering remain only poetry so long as these hopes are not joined to what is politically and technically possible today. Without the "art of the possible," "the art of hope" becomes the opium of the people. A political theology of hope must thus join its visions of the future with the research into what is possible today and relate both to human beings for whose hope it wants to become accountable.

With these premises in mind, I wish to address myself to the influence of biomedical progress upon man and society, and conversely also to the influence of man and society upon biomedical progress.

II. KNOWLEDGE AND INTEREST

Whenever science and ethics are separated, ethics always comes too late. Ethics thus would make us responsible for power only after science has taught us the methods of power. After facts and data have been enumerated, ethics would interpret them to man.

This line of discussion only leads to a deadend. Since we are technically better equipped from year to year to achieve what we want, the helpless ethical question arises: What do we actually want?[3] The more possible futures there are, the less people seem able to agree on a commonly desirable future.

I shall therefore try to reverse the approach. We shall begin with an analysis of the existing ethos of biomedical progress and then question the reaction of this progress on its own ethos.

Only when the interests leading to knowledge of science and the interests leading to the application of humane techniques are discovered is it possible to inquire intelligently into the reciprocal effects of interest and knowledge under present-day conditions.

The segregation of science and society, science and the humanities, technology and ethics has been, and still is, necessary in order to free science in research and application from the limits of existing social, religious, and moral systems, as well as from social ideologies. The memory of the conflicts between the church and science in the cases of Galileo and Darwin is still alive. The conflicts between nationalist Marxism and science in the USSR show that this liberation is also necessary under other circumstances.

The integration of science and society is, however, just as necessary today in order to free the sciences from their new, almost religious, roles into which they have fallen through the supposed segregation (= sanctification) of social interests and systems of values (the "scientific community" and the "non-scientific" community). If priests in earlier times kept sovereign knowledge from the laity, experts now do this today, but the laity remain the same. This allocation of roles is an obstacle to progress. It places too much responsibility on the scientist and leaves the layman subjected to the horror and fascination of science. The task of science can only be to reveal possibilities of decision and consequences of decision which would not otherwise be recognizable. It is therefore itself dependent on the scientific-political and scientific-ethical dialogue from which the consensus of leading interests, values, and priorities of value can be gained.

Science, in research and application, is the execution of a commission. Human interests precede it, are connected with it and incorporated into its progress. So long as these interests are "a matter of course," it is unnecessary to discuss them. Today, however, the morality of "what is a matter of course" has become a problem in many spheres. In the name of what human interests is this progress pursued?

The first human interest in biomedical progress lies in the fight against disease and for health, against death and for longer life.

That sounds obvious so long as man is controlled by natural deficiencies which must be compensated by the achievements of civilization in order for him to survive. It will become a problem, however, when the immediate necessities of life are realized and no longer provide the negative measure for his efforts. What comes after the struggle for existence?

The "struggle for existence" is connected with the elementary interest of man in his personal liberation from dependence of nature in his surroundings and in his own body. It is the other side of his will for power over nature and himself. Since man has become independent of nature, and to the extent to which he becomes powerful over nature, he becomes a "human being," i.e., a person capable of action. Today it is becoming more and more possible for him to determine not only his spiritual and private, but also his physical and social existence. Liberation and power are, however, only of interest so long as one does not have them. The more man gains them, the more questionable becomes the human being who has to plan and live. "What are human beings here for?" At the Ciba-Symposium (1962), Sir Julian Huxley said that after the "struggle for existence," the "striving for fulfillment," i.e., for fulfillment of human possibilities, will come more and more into the foreground.[4] But which possibilities are to be fulfilled and which not? He added that, for mankind, the guidance of the evolution of nature as well as of his own evolution would be the inner determination of his power and freedom. For 3000 years biblical religions have seen in the control of nature the fulfillment of human destiny and yet combined it with the destiny of mankind in the image of the creative God. Man should not be an image of nature or of society and its powers. When this knowledge originated, the possibilities of man were slight while his dependence on impenetrable nature was great. In the course of scientific and technical progress, man—seen positively—can enter into a previously unsuspected realization of these destinies—if he is a "human being."

From the elementary *interests* in liberation and power, a series of *hopes* have arisen in the history of civilization which have been invested in biomedical progress. They are directed toward the improvement of the human condition, the expansion of world understanding, an increase in man's capacity for happiness and the raising of his morality. Based on these hopes, concrete visions have been projected, partly from irony, partly from foolishness: (1) the conquest of virus and other infectious diseases gives rise to the vision of a germ-free world, (2) the development of psychopharmacology is combined with the Utopia of a pain-free life, (3) the incipient technique of organ transplants leads to the idea of replaceable parts of the body and a life without end, and (4) modern eugenics intimates the control and acceleration of the evolution of mankind. It is combined with the vision that "in the future man will create better generations of man."[5]

On the grounds of these interests, hopes, and visions, biomedical progress itself is a magnificent ethical enterprise of man. It remains alive, however, only so long as the interests and hopes of man remain a matter of course.

III. FEEDBACK OF PROGRESS ON ETHICAL INTERESTS

Every human action not only solves existing problems but produces new ones. Things mostly turn out differently from what one had thought. These new problems can be divided into three groups: (1) everything that can be used by man can also be abused by him. That is why biomedical progress is ambivalent so long as man is an unreliable creature, (2) hopes can be disappointed if they cannot be fulfilled, and they can also be disappointed through their fulfillment. Where biomedical utopias are concerned, the problem of the underlying ethics is not the probable impossibility of their realization, but rather their surmised realizability, and (3) any progress in one sphere of life brings the whole system of life out of balance. That is why the balance must always be restored again when progress is only partial. The symbolism of language, legal codes, moral trustworthiness, production conditions must be rearranged.

Point 1 is self-explanatory. I need not expound it. As regards point 2, hopes are generally dashed when something different happens from what one wanted. The liberation of man from his dependence on nature has not only overcome his natural needs, but has also broken through a series of natural, self-regulating systems. These must be replaced by social systems controlled by man.

Biology and medicine have lowered mortality but, on the other hand, they have produced the population explosion. They have overcome a certain natural selection, but have replaced it by a deterioration of the genes. While they fought against bacteria and pests, they created the "silent spring" due to the use of DDT. They subdued pain by drugs and created a world-wide LSD problem. Man's liberation from nature compels the social organization of this freedom, and this has produced an abundance of new social dependencies. The visions of a painless, endless, and improvable life in a germ-free world are abstract if the social, political, and ethical costs of such a world are not taken into account. What was formerly regulated by "nature" by means of disease, early mortality, and selection must now be taken over by social organization: birth control, eugenics, and presumably also passive euthanasia. Encroachment on natural systems must be compensated by substitute achievements. This ecological law probably sets certain limits of toleration in the experiments of man on himself and in his future self-creation if the costs of progress exceed the gains. Biomedical progress is not an automatic guarantee of happiness.

As regards point 3, hopes can, however, also bring disappointment in their fulfillment. Should a pain-free, endless, improvable life in a germ-free world be possible, one hope of mankind is fulfilled while at the same time a dream is lost; for it is questionable what meaning such a life can have and for what purpose such people exist.

Is not a life without pain also a life without love? Is not a life without resistance and struggle also a life without the experience of life? Will not even an endless life be a boring life lacking the character of being once and for all? Monotony, boredom, and lack of experience are already human problems in industrial society which can be suppressed only with difficulty by new psycho-pharmacotherapy and psycho-techniques. The more human interests and hope are fulfilled by biomedical progress, the more the ethical motivations are broken down which propel that progress. People no longer know what they mean when they say "I," or "my body," or "life," or "death." The general interest in this progress can also thereby be weakened and die out. Why should medical progress make men more efficient when most human accomplishments in this society can be formalized and taken over by machines? How can this progress make people capable of being happier if happiness can no longer be defined?

IV. THE CHANGE IN HUMAN INTERESTS

A. *From the Struggle for Existence to the Striving for Fulfillment*

"In the psycho-social evolution, the struggle for existence is substituted by something that could be called the striving for fulfillment. The most important impetus in this phase of evolution is psycho-social pressure."[6] We refer to these fruitful ideas of Julian Huxley in order to characterize the changes in human interests as a result of biomedical progress. In terms of a vision of evolutionary humanism, he described the aim: "The fulfillment of life—greater possibilities of fulfillment in the psychical-spiritual field for more individuals and greater efforts within the community by better utilization of human possibilities and thereby greater pleasure in the abilities of man."[7]

If the struggle for existence is replaced by the striving for fulfillment, the interests and moral systems of men are fundamentally changed. The struggle for existence was a struggle for survival. In it, man was controlled by the threat of the negative lack of food, disease, a hostile environment, and competing groups. The meaning of his life was destined by self-preservation. The more man gains power over hostile nature and his own frail body, however, the less can self-preservation and bare survival be the meaning of his existence. The more he overcomes natural deficiencies and produces an artificial abundance of possibilities, the more life in this abundance of possibilities becomes a problem. The evolution of man therefore extends beyond the negation of negatives in the struggle for existence to planning the positive that should be gained from the profusion of possibilities. So, for the first time, human life in fact has become a moral task.

The more power man obtains, the greater is his responsibility. The interest in self-fulfillment is therefore, of itself, connected with the responsibility for the spheres of nature that can be controlled. And, according to its inner structure "responsibility for something" is always connected with the "responsibility for somebody." The authority before which one must give an account of control thereby exceeds the sphere *for* which one is accountable and is only experienced as something transcendent. I believe that at this point today many experience the "pain of transcendence," which demands responsibility and which, at the same time, avoids the earlier pictures and symbols. This pain of transcendence can be an even more important impulse than "psycho-social pressure." The Jewish-Christian symbol of man as the image of an invisible God in the visible must also be reinterpreted in view of the abundance of power and possibilities of man today if it is to be an effective symbol of his responsibility for the guidance of the evolution of nature and of his genetic experiments with himself.

B.   From "Struggle for Existence" to "Peace in Existence"

If the struggle for existence is replaced by new definitions of human life, those moral systems which have stylized the struggle for existence must be overcome. Forms of life can be developed which, in rational world conditions, make creativity and love possible.

I believe the ethos of the *struggle for existence* must be turned into the ethos of *peace in existence.*

The principle of self-preservation over against others can be turned into the principle of self-realization in others and with others, i.e., the principle of solidarity.

Systems of fear and aggression, which were necessary for self-preservation, can be dismantled in favor of systems of hope and cooperation.

Group-egoism, which arises from self-preservation and leads to struggles for survival and power, threatens mankind with collective suicide today. Even if this can be prevented, this egoism leads to societies that are segregated. Wherever stresses and conflicts occur today, peace will not be attained by reconciliation but by separation, banishment, apartheid, or ghettos. We produce social separations even without racial or class struggles: we send the aged into old-people's homes, the sick into hospitals, the mentally ill into clinics, etc. So the efficient ones and those that have "made it" are by themselves and can share the spoils of the gross social product. According to medical estimates, about fifty per cent of the mentally ill need not be in homes if their families would look after them. But the urban social structure is intolerant.

"Birds of a feather flock together" is how Aristotle described the natural principle of association. This principle has a hostile effect on life in our society today because it produces separation. The principle of recognition of others belongs to the new self-experience and self-fulfillment of man so that dissimilar people can live together and regard their differences and tensions as fruitful. Peace in existence cannot be attained in any other way.

To the ethics of the struggle for existence finally belonged the ideal of health which identified good health with the capacity for work and enjoyment.[8] Good health in the end always amounts to the unimpeded participation in production and an unreduced share in the gross social product. Illness and old age are then only evils which must be repressed. The incurably ill and old are treated similarly, to say nothing of the question of where and how death actually takes place in our hospitals. A new assessment of illness, aging, and dying belongs therefore to the ethics of peace in existence. Illness can be just as important a process of learning and of forming a person as a healthy, active life.

After the future-oriented society of "youthfulness" has been raised from the comic to the ideal, it is time to rediscover the dignity of age. After death has been regarded as a tiresome mischief-maker, there are reasons for learning the art of dying again. The fight against illness and for health is meaningful only then, when it prepares man to become open to the human pain of love and to the productive conflicts of life and death in order to be able to assimilate them humanely. The ethics of the struggle for existence would otherwise lead to a sick society. Where this fight is successful to a certain degree today, it often leads to a stagnation of life and to a passive consumer attitude toward life without any passion. Where it continues, it leads to societies of affluence in a sea of societies of misery on the earth. Only when the ethic of the struggle for existence is overcome by an ethic of "peace in existence" does it happen that the healthy learn from the ill, the young from the old, the living from the dying, and the rich nations from the poor nations, each showing interest in the others and experiencing solidarity from this interest of others.

V. THE RIGHT TO LIVE AND THE RIGHT TO DIE

Biomedical progress has broken through a series of natural systems and made them accessible for man's intervention. These systems must be replaced by social systems regulated by man. We therefore speak of a population politics, a politics of health; and we will also have to connect the new genetics with the word *politics*. Disturbed natural equilibriums must be replaced by social regulations. Life, therefore, will be more conscious. Birth and death, the content and concept of life are no longer matters of course, but must be understood by man in order to be dealt with meaningfully. This takes place in linguistic symbolism, legal settlements, and a new morality.[9]

A.   *The Ego and the Body*

The self-consciousness of man shows itself in the fact that he can say "I" and thereby mean himself. He says, "I am *somebody"* and thereby identifies himself bodily. How is that possible with regard to progress in body medicine and organ transplantation? Since it has been theoretically possible to isolate disease from sick people and to control the whole causal chain of pathogenic agents leading up to all the important conditions in the progress of disease, controlled therapy has become possible. That, however, presupposes setting a distance between the ego and the corporeality it is, as the body that it has. The spontaneous bodily identity of man is replaced by a distanced relationship of property of man to his body. When, however, organs of this body—like parts of the engine in the car he owns—can be replaced, an ego diffusion occurs. What does the symbol "I" then denote: the bodily existence or my body, or an interchangeable set of parts of the physical system? The appropriation of the replaced parts also belongs to organ transplants, as in the case of a prothesis. This does not only apply to the body which must accept and integrate what is at first a foreign part, but also to the ego as the organizing center of the body. To the difficult medical process of the objectification of the body as body belongs, conversely, the difficult and lengthy process of the subjectification of the body as the body of the "I." The isolation of disease from sick people is, for its part, left to the integration of the disease and recovery by these very same people. Medical changes in the body, and especially any possible genetic change in the *conditio humana,* depend on the truth that the object at its disposal is a subject and must remain so, or should. That sets the aims and certain limits of the corresponding surgical operations. If these medical threads can no longer be humanly assimilated by the person concerned and no longer absorbed by his personality, they will be useless from the human point of view. Progress in medical technique concerned with the body must therefore be balanced by the development of an increased sensibility of the "I" if it is to be humanly assimilated. Today it is already an ethical problem for many to find the correct balance between being a body and having a body. If the "I" can no longer be bodily incarnated but must keep its body permanently at the distance of interchangeability of certain parts of the body, an indifference toward the bodily life of oneself and of others arises. It is true that experience of the self as a manipulable thing makes one invulnerable in a certain way, but it also makes one incapable of loving and unproductive. The more invulnerability and painlessness become possible, the more one should sensitize persons' vulnerability through the significant human pains of love. The application and use of medicines find their limitations in the threatening lack of feeling in man. Self-consciousness previously given by corporeality will therefore become a personal task. One must search consciously for one's bodily and social incarnations and knowingly enter the risk of one's vulnerability.

B.   *Life and Experienced Life*

A second linguistic symbol is "life." In the struggle for existence, life means survival. Today, survival can be extended very far and death can be protracted. People can be kept alive without their being conscious of it. It therefore becomes questionable what we mean when we say "life." For medicine, which is obliged to maintain life, it is however very necessary to know—at least in broad outlines—what can be called human life. One can no longer depend on life being a matter of course, something to be taken and given without any human assistance. The more man is able to determine the fate of man, the more he needs a human definition of life. This is especially precarious in the control of birth and death but it is just as problematic as regards what lies in between. Without shrugging off the dangerous practical questions and legal problems, I should like to suggest a provisional definition for discussion: human life is accepted, loved, and experienced life.

Where life cannot be accepted, loved, and experienced, we are no longer dealing with human life. If a child does not feel that he is accepted, he becomes ill. If a person does not accept himself, he loses his vigor. If a life can no longer be experienced, it is dead. One can furthermore say that being human (*homo-esse*) is being interested (*inter-esse*). It is lively as long as it takes part in other life and experiences interest from other life. Indifference and apathy can therefore be called "dead life." Poverty of experience, apathy, and lack of interest in life are spreading to a frightening extent in industrial societies and societies that are medically well provided for.

The monotony of apathetic life is a disease which can no longer be cured technically, but only by overcoming the uniform civilizations we have produced by cultural variety, by associating with people different from us, and the conscious acceptance of pain brought about by differences and conflicts. Experienced life is a life that contains contradiction and finds the strength to include contradictions in itself and to endure them.

C. *Family Planning and Birth Control*

As a result of recent medical knowledge and means, the birth of a child is no longer a mere matter of nature but also of the freedom and responsibility of man. Thanks to the "pill," sexual union for love can be separated from that for reproduction. The begetting and birth of a child has thereby become a moral and social question. To the birth of a child belongs the conscious will and the accepted responsibility for the child. So long as parents live consciously as members of a community, they have also accepted the responsibility for the community as well as the responsibility for their children. Conversely, the community also participates in the responsibility for the children. Not only the biological conception and parturition belong to the life of a child but, of equal importance, is acceptance by the parents and the community. The right to life is therefore no longer an actuality of nature but a task to be shared by the parents and the community. From this arises the right of birth control by the parents and the community. Certain laws regarding eugenics could also arise later although these presuppose that society is "humane," the selection criteria of which would refute the previously established suspicion of the abuse of power. If laws must also be conceded to society as a result of birth-control, the conscious acceptance of children by society must also be expected. One can thus no longer build towns hostile to children. This would finally entail a cautious deprivatizing of families without dissolving the inevitable personal relations between children and parents. If we proceed with the assumption that human life is *accepted life*, then these questions are more important than the questions about the time of the beginning of human life which are still important as regards abortion, but which progress in family planning will make superfluous.

D. The Death of the Body—the Death of a Person

Today it is difficult to determine the definite end of life because a person can be survived by organs of his body. The differentiation of the death of various organs has made the borderline between life and death unclear. There are people whose brain has ceased to function after a protracted heart failure, but where the heart and respiration have taken up their functions again, the body continues to live an unconscious life, but it is a life that is unable to experience anything. Because the brain's inability to function is regarded as being irreversible according to the present state of knowledge, the death of the brain empirically can be regarded as the actual symbol for the end of human life. With it, the human person ceases to exist, even if certain organs can be kept alive.

If, from the biological point of view, the borderline between life and death is indistinct and death loses its clear definition according to the state of medical knowledge and ability, it will become all the more important to understand death humanely as being the death of the whole person and, by conscious attitudes toward death, to integrate it in experienced life. Death can certainly be determined by the atrophy of certain vital organs, but it is experienced by man in the love which embodies the soul and animates the body. The more we incarnate ourselves in love, the more vulnerable we are by death, the death of those we love and by our own death. Conversely, the more interest in life fades, the less we feel grief and pain because we have already psychologically anticipated death. With the help of drugs, many people today have developed techniques of no longer having to experience life in case of the actual event of death: techniques of indifference and apathy. An ethic of accepted, loved, and experienced life must, for its part, practice attitudes toward death and liberate dying from its repression or glamorization. As life and love are an art, the ability to die is also an art. We indeed know, in the double sense, how one can "take life" but we know very little about how one can leave it humanly and with dignity. Man has a right to his own death in the same way that he has a right to his life. The medical possibilities of removing the dividing line between life and death and making it unconscious, will then be humanely used, if one prepares oneself for death and, more consciously than formerly, surrenders to it when the time comes. This other attitude toward death demands a process of education that removes the barriers of repression over against death and grief so that life again becomes worthy of love.

Just because biomedial progress elicits hopes, and yet does not contain a guarantee of happiness, it must be guided by a humane ethics which ought to lead from the struggle for existence to peace in existence, if human evolution is not to end in the *nihil*. A political theology of hope cannot merely develop a poetry of feelings, but must serve the practical and political as well as the personal shaping of a new life-style. This appears to me to be more important than enthusiasm or *Weltschmerz*.

NOTES

[1]Charles A. Reich, *The Greening of America* (New York: Random House, 1970), pp. 287 ff.

[2]Willy Brandt, "Eine Politik für den Menschen—Phrase oder Programm?" in *Evangelische Kommentare*, 4 (1971), 474.

[3]Bertrand de Jouvenel, "Political Science and Prevision," *American Political Science Review*, 59 (1965), 30. Cf. also Ossip Kurt Flechtheim, *History and Futurology* (Meisenheim am Glan: K.G. Anton Hain, 1966).

[4]*Man and His Future*, Ciba Foundation Symposium (Boston: Little, Brown, 1963); German version: *Das umstrittene Experiment Mensch: Elemente einer biologischen Revolution* (München, 1966), p. 47.

[5]*Ibid.*, p. 289.   [6]*Ibid.*, p. 47.   [7]*Ibid.*, p. 33.

[8]Sigmund Freud, cited in J. Scharffenberg, *Religion zwischen Wahn und Wirklichkeit* (Hamburg, 1972), p. 116.

[9]Cf. Leon R. Kass, "The New Biology: What Price Relieving Man's Estate?" *Science*, 174 (1971), 779 ff.

Response to Jürgen Moltmann

CHRISTOPHER F. MOONEY, S.J.

The provocative paper which we heard from Professor Moltmann is a good instance, I think, of a modern theologian seeking to grapple with some of the cultural implications of his own theological thought. The area he has chosen, that of ethical decision, is a significant one, since the theology he has helped fashion these last few years does indeed impinge upon man's human hopes for biomedical progress, as well as upon the political choices he must make when faced with the possible futures offered him by scientific research. My own role is to comment upon what Professor Moltmann has said from the viewpoint of the future-oriented, evolutionary system of Pierre Teilhard de Chardin. From this viewpoint I have only one comment, and it is intended to complete rather than to correct what he has written.

In his paper Professor Moltmann expressed a genuine concern for those interests men have in fighting disease as well as the hopes they entertain for biomedical progress. He seems to presume, however, that such interests and hopes will always be there, and that the Christian problem is how to prevent their abuse, how to channel them in such a way that they will promote life, not death, and furthermore, as he well says, not simply life, but life accepted, loved, and experienced. The more fundamental question, however, is whether scientific research, biomedical or any other, is going to continue at all. Long before recent diagnoses, Teilhard de Chardin located our present crisis in a loss of nerve. For large numbers, the arrival of the future has been accelerated to an alarming degree, and growing technological control appears to be either an invitation to self-destruction or a headlong return to the regimentation of the anthill. The more basic problem, therefore, is not the prospect of boredom and monotony in a germ-free, pain-free world, but whether there is going to be anyone who still wants to strive for such a world. "O man of the twentieth century," Teilhard once asked, "how does it happen that you are waking up to horizons and are susceptible to fears that your forefathers never knew? . . . Here only, at this turning point where the future substitutes itself for the present . . . do our perplexities legitimately and indeed inevitably begin. Tomorrow? But who can guarantee us a tomorrow anyway? And without the assurance that this tomorrow exists, can we really go on living, we to whom has been given . . . the terrible gift of foresight? Sickness of the dead end. . . . This time we have at last put our finger on the tender spot."[1]

It is this tender spot, namely the growing suspicion that he has nowhere to go in the universe, which is causing modern man to ask whether or not he has been duped by life. An animal may rush headlong down a blind alley or toward a precipice, but man, precisely because he can reflect on his condition, will no longer continue to take steps in a direction he knows to be blocked. In spite of growing control over material energy and biomedical sciences, in spite of greater awareness of responsibility, in spite of the pressures of immediate needs and desires, without a taste for life mankind will simply stop inventing and constructing. This explains why the fundamental law of morality for Teilhard is to liberate that conscious energy which seeks further to unify the world. This energy he calls "the zest for life," that disposition of mind and heart that relishes the experience of life and manifests itself particularly in the enthusiasm a man has for creative tasks undertaken from a sense of duty. Only such a zest for life, he felt, can overcome that existential fear that has arisen from man's sudden realization that he is now gaining control of the evolutionary process. The task before him, he has become aware, is "to seize the tiller of the world," to take hold of all those energies by which he has reached his present position and to use them to move ahead. For only by cultivating this moral sense of obligation to life is he going to be able to avoid either ecological disaster or nuclear destruction.

This is a problem, we should note, not of the oppressed groups of the world or of any particular group at all, but of man as a whole. In fact, the oppressed are less likely just now to despair of life than are their oppressors. At least it is clear to the oppressed that the meaning of their lives is to fight the oppressors, and their anger is making this an easy thing to do. Those who are in control of the world's resources, however, whether political, economic, or cultural are becoming less and less sure of what to do with the control they possess, and more and more afraid of that upheaval all around them which they try in vain to understand.

Although Teilhard speaks frequently of man's struggle for existence, he actually understands this phrase in much the same sense as the phrase Professor Moltmann uses: "peace in existence," namely an ethos which makes it possible for man to develop his capacity for love and creativity. Teilhard would likewise agree with Dr. Moltmann that this search of man for psycho-spiritual fulfillment involves "the pain of transcendence" and implies an authority before which one must give an account how one has used one's power. This is why Teilhard's explanation of man's present experience is so intimately linked to the Christian message of universal love and the community of all men with the person of Jesus. Teilhard says quite explicitly that the ultimate grounds for man's hope in the future *have* to be religious, since such grounds alone can provide the strong ethical drive to act in the present crisis, as well as that assurance that Someone is helping us transcend our own limitations. Without this assurance, human love alone simply cannot motivate mankind, since each man is forced by life to acknowledge the frailty of his own love. Unless some divine power strengthens this human love and supports human freedom, the ultimate success of the human enterprise will forever remain doubtful and insecure. As a Christian, Teilhard saw the ultimate source of this love in the person of Christ, who by his incarnation, death, and resurrection has conquered man's native tendency toward repulsion and isolation. For only what God has done in Christ can bring assurance that man's creativity is indeed a participation in God's creativity, and that the outcome will therefore be on the side of life and not on the side of death. Teilhard's total system is thus clearly a Christology, and his natural theology is very much only a part of this larger whole.

Nevertheless, we must recognize that this hope of Teilhard was not vision. In Christianity he saw rational invitations to an act of faith in the future. His whole life was an affirmation of that faith in spite of all the discouragement which came from the obvious failures and stupidity of man. "It is a terrifying thing to have been born," he wrote once. "I mean to find oneself, without having willed it, swept irrevocably along on a torrent of fearful energy which seems as though it wished to destroy everything it carries with it."[2] The terror experienced by men today as they take responsibility for the future was thus a terror experienced by Teilhard himself. Through Christ, however, he saw that a new impulse of hope was possible and was now beginning to take shape in human consciousness. This hope was that the time-space totality of evolution would be immortalized and personalized in Christ to the extent that it would become lovable. This is why he could pray: "What I want, my God, is that by a reversal of forces which you alone can bring about, my terror in face of the nameless changes destined to renew my being may be turned into an overflowing joy at being transformed into you."[3] Like all men whose hope is strong, Teilhard cherished every sign of new life and was ready at any moment to help the birth of that which is ready to be born. Yet he was a man who hoped in the midst of doubt, doubt which—like the sufferings of men—he recognized as the price and condition for the perfection of the universe. And under these conditions he was content to walk right to the end along a road of which he was more and more certain toward an horizon more and more shrouded in mist.

NOTES

[1]Pierre Teilhard de Chardin, *The Phenomenon of Man,* revised English edition (New York: Harper & Row, 1965), pp. 228-229.

[2]Pierre Teilhard de Chardin, *Hymn of the Universe,* tr. Simon Bartholomew (New York: Harper & Row, 1965), p. 29.

[3]*Ibid.*

Response to
Jürgen Moltmann

SCHUBERT M. OGDEN

In the original announcement of this meeting, it was described as a "two-stage conference." We were told that the American Teilhard de Chardin Association is projecting a second conference, which would build on the present one by bringing the three groups of theologians represented here into dialogue with "future planners," i.e., "scientists, technologists, sociologists, and political scientists." To this extent, then, Professor Moltmann is certainly justified in observing at the beginning of his paper that "our conference is intended not only theologically and philosophically to clarify the concepts *hope* and *future,* but also to develop desirable and realizable *models* of the future" (p. 89). But, more than that, it seems to me he has placed us all in his debt by anticipating just the kind of second-stage discussion for which the present stage has been planned as the preparation. By focusing on the biomedical future of man and suggesting at least the outlines of "a humane ethics," he has helped develop a model not only for the human future itself but also for the further, more empirical and scientific discussion of that future, which our efforts here can only show to be all the more desirable.

Keeping in mind our primary intention at this first stage, however, I wish to limit my response to his paper to some of the more strictly theological or philosophical issues it has seemed to me to raise. Such a limitation is further justified, I believe, because Professor Moltmann himself evidently intends his paper to be a theological, or possibly, philosophical-theological contribution. Furthermore, I think he would agree with me that, if we theologians and philosophers have anything distinctive to contribute to this whole discussion, it can only lie in the relative adequacy of our distinctively theological and philosophical claims. Even so, given the rather broader scope of his paper, much of which is involved in more empirical or scientific kinds of questions, my limited response to it cannot hope to do justice to everything it sets before us.

I.

The first issue I take the paper to raise is the more formal, methodological issue of the nature and task of theology. Let me say right at the outset that I am well aware that clarification of this issue is not a major concern of this paper and that others of Professor Moltmann's many writings may quite legitimately be referred to as amplifying its discussion here. The fact remains that he expressly addresses himself to this question; and, for reasons already given, it seems to me important to consider what he says.

His main point, as I get it, is expressed by the descriptive phrase, "a political theology of hope" (pp. 91, 104), by which he seems to mean a complex undertaking having at least two main aspects or functions: (1) "a religious symbolism of anxiety and hope" (pp. 90-91), hence the function "to afford symbolic expression of the contemporary religious sensibility" (p. 89), and (2) "a political initiative in the conflicts of the present" (p. 91), hence the function to "serve the practical and political as well as the personal shaping of a new life-style" (p. 104). In its first aspect or function, theology is said, somewhat vaguely, to be *"involved in* the 'culture' of our sensibility" and *"belong to* the public poetry of the fundamental sensibility of its age" (p. 89, my italics); and, in the second, it is said, also somewhat vaguely, to "share in and cooperate with the presence of the future in scientific progress and politico-ethical decisions" (p. 91). At one point, passing reference is also made to what would appear to be a more strictly hermeneutical task for theology, namely, in the reference to the need for a reinterpretation of "the Jewish-Christian symbol of man as the image of an invisible God in the visible." But, significantly, perhaps, the only criterion for such reinterpretation even suggested at this point is that the symbol thereby be rendered "effective," i.e., "an effective symbol of [man's] responsibility for the guidance of the evolution of nature and of his genetic experiments with himself" (pp. 97-98).

Now, realizing that rather different things have been, and quite properly are, meant by the word "theology," I can only confess that I have difficulties with this understanding of theology's nature and task. My first and greatest difficulty is that I find no indication here that the primary, because most distinctive, function of theology is critical—that it is, above all, a fully reflective undertaking whose characteristic concern is with the fundamental questions of meaning and truth. On my view, in contrast to Professor Moltmann's, theology may be said to have expressive and practical functions, or, if you will, to *be* "a religious symbolism" and to *be* "a political initiative," in an *indirect* sense only. Insofar as it is the critical interpretation of religious symbols, theology is also, in its way, expressive of the "religious sensibility"; and, by the same token, it also has, in its way, a practical relevance, since it is ultimately ordered to the same practical or existential end as the "religious sensibility" itself.

But, in both respects, the way of theology, as befits a properly critical, reflective, interpretative undertaking, is indirect: it is not so much poetry as poetic criticism, and it is a political initiative in somewhat the sense political science and political philosophy are.

Closely connected with this, then, is my second difficulty that theology, as Professor Moltmann here speaks of it, seems to have next to nothing to do with the critical interpretation of the specifically Christian witness of faith. Again, the question I am raising is not simply how we are to make use of the word "theology." Call it what you will, from the time of the New Testament onward, there has been, and I trust will continue to be, the hermeneutical task of critically interpreting the witness of faith or "kerygma" of the specifically Christian community, as something distinctively different from the "contemporary religious sensibility." Among the other things this has meant, and I hope will continue to mean, is that the terms of this theological task have by no means been set solely or even primarily by the fact that, as Professor Moltmann says, "sensibilities change" (p. 90). Clearly, the theology of hope is not alone in having, as he says, "an historical context" for its origins and for the wide response to it (p. 89); and we may agree, I think, that it would be a poor theology indeed that did not continually struggle to render its claims understandable, which is to say, meaningful and true, given the limitations and opportunities of its particular cultural situation. But, surely, if theological revision is called for, it is not only or even primarily because "the hopes of the 1960's have 'gone with the wind,'" and "words like 'frustration' and 'betrayal' . . . apparently are becoming keywords of our present *Lebensgefühl*" (p. 90). Nor, I should think, is the sole criterion of such theological reinterpretation as may be necessary effectiveness, unless by that is meant really only appropriateness to the witness of the Christian community or understandability to the contemporary hearer, given defensible standards of meaning and truth.

II.

The second kind of issue I find Professor Moltmann raising is more material in that it pertains directly to the first-order questions of theological ethics and anthropology. You will recall that his guiding concern in the paper is to contribute to the development of "models" of the human future that are: (1) "desirable"; and (2) "realizable" (p. 89). I take it that he intends his own reflections on "an ethic of accepted, loved, and experienced life" (p. 104), or on an ethic organized around "the principle of self-realization in others and with others" rather than on "the principle of self-preservation" (p. 98), to make this kind of a contribution. But, if this assumption is correct, I see at least three points of difficulty in his argument.

The first has to do with what, exactly, is to be understood by "desirable." So far as I can see, Professor Moltmann either fails sufficiently to clarify how he uses this concept or else is content with an analysis that I, at least, find inadequate. Ordinarily, "what is desirable" cannot be identified forthwith with "what is desired," any more than "what is believable" (in the sense of "credible" or "true") can be supposed to be the same as "what is believed." And yet, when one looks at what little the paper has to say on this question, "what is desirable" seems to mean either simply what is in fact "desired" (p. 91), or what we "actually want" (p. 92), or, yet again, what is the object of "the consensus of leading interests, values, and priorities of value" (p. 93). I press this question without prejudice as to how a complete analysis of "desirable" ought to be carried out. In fact, as a Christian theologian and a theist, I strongly suspect that the ordinary distinction between the "desirable" and the "desired" can no more be applied to the extraordinary case of God, even analogically, than can that between the "believable" (or "true") and the "believed." Even so, I see no reason to suppose that it does not have a valid and very important application to the ordinary case of man and his moral decisions, and I find it puzzling that Professor Moltmann should suppose that the question, "What do we actually want?" is, in any direct way, at least, an "*ethical* question" (p. 92; my italics).

The second point of difficulty has to do with whether, or in what sense, the proposed model of man's future is "realizable." That "a humane ethics," as Professor Moltmann says, "*ought to* lead from the struggle for existence to peace in existence, if human evolution is not to end in the *nihil*" (p. 104; my italics) I have no trouble believing; nor do I see any reason to doubt his virtually tautological statement that "peace in existence cannot be attained in any other way" than by accepting "the principle of recognition of others" (pp. 98-99). But from statements such as this about what *ought to be*, or, in a conditional sense, *must be* if the project man is not to fail (cf. p. 98), I see no valid way of inferring the truth of statements about what actually *can be*. Yet what other warrant does Professor Moltmann give us for the several such statements he apparently makes, e.g., "Forms of life *can be* developed which, in rational world conditions, make creativity and love possible"; or "The principle of self-preservation over against others *can be* turned into the principle of self-realization in others and with others"; or, again, "Systems of fear and aggression, which were necessary for self-preservation, *can be* dismantled in favor of systems of hope and cooperation" (p. 98, my italics)? What kind of a "can be" is being asserted here? Are these all merely possibilities in principle, or are they also, as they certainly seem to be, possibilities in fact? And if they are the latter, in what sense is this so? What, specifically, are the factual conditions that make them possible, and what reasons do we have for supposing that these conditions are or eventually will be fulfilled? I fear I also find it not a little hard to understand how Professor Moltmann can assert such possibilities as genuinely factual and yet also speak as though he has left the optimism of the 1960's far behind him, or call for "a revision of hope theology" that would have to take note of "the problems of radical evil, [of] the absurdity of misdirected evolutionary processes, of death and the tragedy of human existence in order to arrive at an expression of solid human hope" (p. 90).

Which brings me to the third point of difficulty—and the last thing I wish to say in this response. Where I suspect virtually all of my differences from Professor Moltmann have their origin is in our sharply different understandings of the nature and destiny of man. I have just referred to what I can only regard as his much too optimistic assessment of the future of man in history, and this is one example of the sort of difference I have in mind. But there are any number of other examples that might also be developed. Take his claim that "hope for a new and different future is possible *only* among the suffering and the oppressed" (p. 91; my italics). Unless the phrase, "the suffering and the oppressed," is to be taken in so loose and improper a sense that this claim becomes trivially true, it seems to me there are good reasons for thinking it false. As a matter of fact, Professor Moltmann himself unintentionally adduces such reasons when he appeals elsewhere in the paper to Julian Huxley's distinction between "struggle for existence" and "striving for fulfillment." Huxley's intention in making this distinction, as I recall, is much the same as Whitehead's, when he suggests that the explanation of "the active attack on the environment," which in some way is characteristic not only of man but of all "higher forms of life," is "a three-fold urge: (i) to live, (ii) to live well, (iii) to live better."[1] My point is not at all that those who suffer from present conditions do not have a special interest in radically changing them; they obviously do. But suffering is certainly not the only reason for such interest, since man simply as man is the being who consciously lives in the realm of possibilities and ideals that always beckon him beyond the security of present attainment. As Reinhold Niebuhr once put it in a memorable simile, the condition of man is "the condition of the sailor climbing the mast, with the abyss of the waves beneath him and the 'crow's nest' above him. He is anxious about both the end toward which he strives and the abyss of nothingness into which he may fall."[2]

But where I find myself furthest from Professor Moltmann is in what he seems to understand by man's relation to nature. It is striking that the characteristic use of the word "nature" throughout his paper is in such locutions as "*hostile* nature" or "*impenetrable* nature" (pp. 97, 94; my italics) and that what he calls "the achievements of civilization" are represented as compensating for "natural deficiencies" (p. 93)—as though there could even be such a thing as civilization apart from man's capacities to acquire culture and to make use of symbolic language, both of which are eminently "natural" because genetically conditioned! We are also told that becoming a "human being" is a matter of becoming "independent of nature" and "powerful over nature" (p. 93)—as though such independence and power as man can attain could ever be anything other than eminently "natural" gifts freely bestowed by "the grace of nature" by which he alone can live! Of course, Professor Moltmann may be right in saying that "for 3000 years biblical religions have seen in the control of nature the fulfillment of human destiny and yet combined it with the destiny of mankind in the image of the creative God" (p. 94). But some of us, at least, are not yet convinced of this, and we seem to see signs in the biblical witness itself that those of our contemporaries are not wholly wrong who attribute to a peculiarly "Christian heresy" that desanctification of nature and life which has progressively led to their profanation. In any case, the evidence mounts all around us—in our cities and fields, in our streams and oceans—that theology today has no more urgent a task than to think this question through all the way to the bottom. For whether man is to have any future at all on this planet may well depend on his rapidly acquiring another and very different understanding of himself in relation to the nature whose nature is also his nature and with whose destiny his own is inextricably bound.

NOTES

[1] Alfred North Whitehead, *The Function of Reason* (Princeton: Princeton University Press, 1929), p. 51.

[2] Reinhold Niebuhr, *The Nature and Destiny of Man*, Vol. I (New York: Charles Scribner's Sons, 1949), p. 185.

The Future Ex Memoria Passionis

JOHANNES B. METZ

I. THE SOCIO-POLITICAL TOPOS

"Even the future is no more what it was before." And in fact, confidence in a supposed gradual evolution of technological civilization has vanished. If "progress" exists at all, it occurs now only in opposition to a naive generalization about it. The warm stream of teleology that has supported us till now is increasingly drying up. Teleological reliance on a growing reconciliation between man and nature is now broken; and with its disappearance we notice for the first time the deep tenacious grasp it had on us—a grasp reaching even into the philosophical and theological interpretations we made concerning the future. But now there suddenly appears again beside Prometheus, Sisyphus; beside Marx, Nietzsche; beside Teilhard, Camus and Monod.

We are becoming more and more clearly aware of the dangers and antagonisms which arise when technological and economic processes are left to themselves and political and social systems of control break down: dying cities, destroyed environmental systems, exploding populations, the chaos in information, the increasingly aggressive and vicious spiralling of the conflict between North and South, leading possibly in its turn to a new escalation in the power struggle between East and West; etc., etc. In addition to this, there is the threat posed to man's self-identity and freedom by the growing possibilities of psychological and genetic manipulation. In addition, one may suspect that, once left to itself, the technological-economic planning of man's future is going to produce the totally accommodated and conformist human being: a man whose dreams and fantasies can no longer keep pace and are choked in the functionalism of the technical apparatus; a man whose freedom degenerates into the simple adaptibility instinctive to all animals whereby they conform to the superior strength and complexity of preformed behavior patterns; a man whose sensitivity to the unmanageability of the world has been so blunted that the horizon of his living has been robbed of risk. A future of man realized according to these purely technological-economic principles would seem to foreshadow the disappearance of man as that being who has nourished himself on the historical substance of his freedom, on the power, namely, which finds alternative possibilities even within the process of accommodation. And this is why voices are raised today which follow up Nietzsche's announcement of the Death of God with the further proclamation of the Death of Man, a death manifesting itself in the paralysis of his spontaneity and his interment in the grave of a technical-economic structuralism. The fear arises that man's very thinking is losing its dialectical power to confront and challenge an established order and is being integrated into a nameless, all-encroaching process of production.

This situation seems to me to prevent any discussion of the future in general categories, divorced from any subject, categories like development, progress, or even "process." Rather, one should be asking: *whose* development, *whose* progress, the process proper to *which* subject? We have to ask about the *goal* of development, progress, and process. The question of the future of our technological civilization is not primarily a problem within technology, but rather the question of how we use technology and technological-economic processes. It is not primarily a question of means but of ends, of establishing priorities and preferences. This means, however, that the problem is primarily a political and, fundamentally, a social problem.

But how can politics become the primary *topos* for the question about the future in our technological society? Are we not witnessing the death struggle of a politics autonomous over against technology and economics? Isn't there a growth in the anonymous dictatorship of structures and processes which makes the dictatorship of persons and parties seem harmless by comparison? Kenneth Boulding writes: "We can conceive of a world where an invisible dictatorship is still making use of democratic forms of government." Does not our technological society bring about the progressive euthanasia of politics? Are we not seeing the increasing self-paralysis of political reason and its degeneration into an instrumental reason serving technological and economic processes and their anonymous power systems? How are we to find a politics capable of regulating these systems and extricating them from the contradictions and catastrophes appearing today?

Would we be helped here by some kind of radical scientification of politics? Certainly, in the pursuit of its own ends, political life is becoming steadily less capable of doing without the mediation and mobilization of scientific knowledge. It is not science, however, that will constitute and guarantee the authenticity of political consciousness over against technological controls. For our modern sciences are themselves technological in an essential and not simply incidental way, and this relationship is a presupposition for their success and is grounded in their specific mode of knowledge, knowledge as the domination of nature. Insofar as this form of knowing dominates in a society certain fundamental experiences—such as the experiences of suffering, of sorrow, or of pain—are functionally devalued, losing their original cognitive and critical character. This, of course, raises a vast number of questions which cannot be pursued any further here. Just one remark: a politics which is to be more than simply a successful accommodation to the systems of technical and economic processes is rooted in something greater and other than science (as we know and understand it today).

It is obvious that this kind of politics will only come to be when our political life has itself undergone a fundamental change. No transposition of politics into a purely technological administration and a computer-politics is going to help; these simply reproduce the difficulties mentioned without providing a solution. Equally untenable would be an old-style decision-politics or Machiavellianism, a kind of stone-age politics in the twentieth century. What is ultimately demanded of us here is a new form of political life and new political structures. Only when this succeeds are human cultures going to be possible in the future at all. And in this sense, politics becomes indeed the new name for culture (and, again in this sense, every theology attempting to reflect on Christian traditions in the context of the world's problems becomes "political theology"). I would like now to mention certain elements proper to this new orientation of political life and show the kind of structural pattern it is assuming.

Our situation demands a new connection between politics and morals, one which refuses to be content with that kind of trivial morality typical of an affluent society and still preserved for us in the liberal separation of politics and morals. As Habermas says:

> There are indications that developed social systems already accept, or are on the point of accepting, certain international imperatives of life—namely, the elimination of war as a legitimate means of settling conflicts and the removal of mass poverty and disparities in economic development. Even where these systems do not produce at present adequate motives for the solution of such global problems, one thing is nevertheless already clear: a solution to these problems is hardly possible without applying throughout public life those universalist norms which were hitherto required only in the private sphere. Someone still tied to the old categories might call this the moralization of politics. But this kind of idea should not already be dismissed simply on those grounds as naive enthusiasm.

This new connection between politics and morals cannot be ordained from above, nor can it be allowed to relapse into the political canonization of a particular moral system, nor seek to realize a totalitarian identification of political and ethical practice. It demands the mobilization of the spiritual and moral powers in society through a radical process of democratizing the infra-structures and grassroots, i.e., by nourishing from below freedom and efficient responsibility in society.

The kind of political life which would bring about a culture of freedom within technological-economic processes cannot, in my opinion, afford to ignore those reserves of moral and political imagination being developed in the present subcultures and countercultures of our technological society. Far more is implied in this "Youth Culture" than the usual generation conflict. It is in a certain sense our Western form of cultural revolution, the experiment of seeking an alternative to the systems of our technological society. Anyone waiting for the escapists to troop penitently back like lost sheep into the established system has misunderstood both this culture and his own situation.

Although this new form of political life does not confine its projected aims to what is deemed plausible by the controlling technological-economic forces, it naturally does not intend to bypass technology and economics as such. There is neither an alternative to technology, nor (up till now) an alternative technology. What is sought for and demanded is rather a new mediation, an instrumental control of this technology and these technical and economic processes. One thing above all has to be avoided: the dissolution of political fantasy and political action into the pure and simple business of planning. For only the independence of the political dimension can guarantee the possibility of a human future.

This situation reminds one of the story about the struggle between two giants. One of them is weaker and stands on the brink of defeat. And yet, against all odds, he manages to keep the struggle going and finally frees himself from the clutches of the other. He is able to do this because a tiny humpbacked dwarf is sitting in his giant ear encouraging him and whispering to him again and again new modes of resistance. This story could be a parable for the struggle between technology and politics, between a purely technological-economic planning on the one hand and a political project for the future on the other. Political fantasy will prevent itself from being ultimately absorbed by the restrictive grasp of technology so long as it retains that moral fantasy and power to resist which has grown out of the memory of suffering accumulated throughout history. The dwarf stands for the memory of this suffering: the parallel is apt, for in our advanced social systems suffering is in fact pictured as insignificant and ugly and better kept out of sight.

Political consciousness *ex memoria passionis*, political action flowing from the memory of mankind's history of suffering: this could indicate an understanding of politics which would lead to new possibilities and new criteria for the mastering of technological and economic processes. It provides inspiration for a new form of solidarity, of responsibility toward those furthest away from us, for the history of suffering unites all men like a "second nature." It prevents any purely technical understanding of freedom and peace; it excludes any form of peace and freedom purchased at the price of the suppressed history of suffering belonging to other peoples and groups. It forces us to look at the public *theatrum mundi* not just from the standpoint of the successful and the well-established, but with the eyes of the conquered and the sacrificed. (In earlier times this was the function of the fool at court: the fool stood for an alternative to the policy of his master, an alternative which had been rejected, overcome, or suppressed. His politics were something like a politics of the memory of suffering—as opposed to the classical political principle of "Woe to the Conquered" and as opposed to the Machiavellian despot. The task confronting us today is to overcome in a new synthesis the "division of labor" in political life between the Powerful and the "Fool" with his powerless imagination of suffering. It is here that I see the significance in a new connection between politics and morals.) And so there finally emerges a conception of political life and political responsibility for which the great moral and religious traditions could possibly be mobilized, once these traditions have been grasped at their deepest level of meaning.

II. NATURE AND HISTORY

Thus the thematic of the future reveals itself as a directly political and fundamentally social problem. In my suggestion, political and social activity directed toward the future discovers its orientation, its "norms," from a motivating context in history and not from a universal theory of nature. But isn't this to place our future once more on unreliable, shaky ground? For if social and political action now establishes the priorities for our technological-scientific-economic development and if this social and political action is nourished and defined by historical consciousness, then isn't our future thus exposed anew to the antagonisms of historical interests and parties? And shouldn't we stop all this rummaging around among the exhausted and exploited mysteries of history? Shouldn't we define our future in terms of a universal theory of nature?

And yet every attempt to reconcile nature and man is utopian in its core and therefore itself historically dialectical in character. There is no teleological, finalistic mediation between nature and man. This seems to be decisively confirmed wherever modern natural science—as in biology—becomes anthropology. One has only to read Monod as opposed to Teilhard and even perhaps Whitehead! Apart from this, however, the fact remains: it is suffering that opposes an affirmative theory of reconciliation between man and nature. Every such attempt at reconciliation degenerates finally into the worst kind of ontologizing of man's torment. Suffering brings out the contrast between nature and history, between teleology and eschatology. There is no "objective" reconciliation of the two, no transparent and manageable unity between them. All such attempts are beneath the dignity of human suffering. And this is particularly blatant wherever the attempt is made to understand human suffering as a modality of a general reciprocity of nature between *actio* and *passio*. This is nothing but a scholasticism of suffering—in both senses of the word! The smallest trace of meaningless suffering in the world we experience gives the lie to this whole affirmative ontology and all our teleology and unmasks them as modern mythology.

The suffering of men resists all attempts to interpret history and historical processes in terms of nature. Presupposed here, of course, is a consciousness of identity which reveals itself negatively in suffering. This identity-consciousness resists any reduction to the trivial identity, let us say, of an oyster which was exactly the same a hundred million years ago as it is on my plate in a New York restaurant today. By this identity-consciousness we do not mean the anthropocentric of power and domination over nature, but rather the anthropocentric of suffering which prevails over against every cosmocentrism. And thus it is not idealistic pride but rather respect for the dignity of the burden of suffering in history which moves us to interpret nature from the viewpoint of history (and this means interpreting the connection between nature and history dialectically and not teleologically), that is, moves us to view the millions of years of Nature's time as an "inflation of time" compared with the time of suffering proper to man.

The substratum of history is not nature as development or as process without a subject. The natural history of man is in a certain sense the history of his passion of suffering. In this understanding of man's history, the absence of reconciliation between nature and man is not suppressed, but preserved—and this over against every teleological projection and every ontological generalization. For this history of suffering has no goal—it has at most a future. And the continuity of this history is not accessible to us through teleologies, but rather through the traces of suffering this history contains. The essential content of history is the memory of suffering as a negative consciousness of future freedom. Once the disparity between man and nature is presupposed, the history of freedom is possible only as the history of suffering. Every conception of the history of freedom as a non-dialectical evolutionary development proves to be abstract and ideological. Or, put another way: the future of freedom can itself only be historically explained. But this binds social and political action by their very nature to historical consciousness and prevents either a stoic withdrawal from the antagonisms of history or a teleological optimism overlooking its contradictions.

III. THE FUTURE OF FREEDOM IN THE MEMORY OF SUFFERING

Christianity does not subsequently introduce God as a kind of stop-gap into this conflict about the future; rather, it attempts to keep the memory of the crucified Lord, this particular *memoria passionis, alive* as a dangerous memory of freedom in the social systems of our technological civilization. This statement requires closer examination and development. I would simply like to mention a few points which seem to me important here.

First of all, a category which I have already used quite frequently in the course of these reflections on the theme of the future must now be explained more precisely: this is the category of *memoria*. What prevents memory from being a traditionalistic, even a reactionary category when we employ it to define future in so fundamental a way? What prevents it from becoming a bourgeois counterposition over against hope, leading us insidiously away from the risks of the future? In what sense can memory function as a practical-critical, yes, even dangerously liberating power? Now there are very different kinds of memories. There are memories in which we simply do not take the past seriously enough: memories where the past becomes for us an unthreatened paradise, a place of refuge from our present disappointments; this is the past of the "good old days." There are memories which bathe everything from the past in a soft, conciliatory glow. "Memory transfigures," we say, and sometimes we experience this rather drastically, for instance when veterans meet in their local bar and exchange stories of their war experiences: the inferno of war is screened out of these memories; what apparently remains is simply the adventure long since overcome! The past goes through the filter of the harmless cliché; everything dangerous, oppressive, and challenging has vanished from it; it seems deprived of all future. Here memory so easily becomes a "false consciousness" of our past and an opiate for our present.

But there is also another kind of memory, dangerous memories, memories which challenge us. These allow earlier experiences to penetrate right into the middle of our lives and as such give rise to new and dangerous insights for the present. They illuminate for an instant in a harsh glare the questionable nature of those things we have apparently come to terms with and they reveal the banality of our supposed "realism." They break through the canon of what prevails everywhere as self-evident and unmask as a deception the certainty of those "whose hour is always at hand." (John 7:6) They sabotage, as it were, the structure of all we consider plausible and have, in this sense, an essentially subversive character. Such memories are like dangerous and incalculable visitations from the past. They are memories we have to reckon with, memories, as it were, with future content. "Remembrance of the past," Herbert Marcuse notes, "can allow dangerous insights to emerge, and the established society seems to fear the subversive content of this memory." It is no accident that a typical method of totalitarian rule is to destroy the memory of the past. Men's slavery in fact begins when their memories of the past are taken away. Every form of colonization is based on this principle. And every revolt against oppression nourishes itself from the subversive strength of remembered suffering. The memory of accumulated suffering continues to resist the modern cynics of political power.

There is an obvious danger today that everything in our consciousness marked by memory, everything outside the calculations of our technical-pragmatic reason will simply be identified with superstition and left to the private whim of the individual. But this doesn't necessarily make us freer and "more enlightened"! We just fall prey to the prevailing illusions more easily and become victims of further manipulation. The examples are legion! In resistance to the modern prophets of the disappearance of history there stands the remembrance of accumulated suffering. This prevents us from understanding history either just as a background setting for an occasional, festive interpretation of our life or simply as distant material for historical criticism. As a remembered history of suffering, history retains the form of a "subversive tradition." This tradition resists any attempt to overcome it and bring it to a halt, either through a purely affirmative attitude toward the past (as given in the hermeneutical theories) or through a purely critical attitude toward the past (as found in ideology-critique). In any event, its mediation is essentially practical in nature.

Christian faith articulates itself as *memoria passionis, mortis et resurrectionis Jesu Christi*. At the center of this faith stands the memory of the crucified Lord, a particular *memoria passionis* on which is grounded the promise of future freedom for all. To say we are reminded of the future of our freedom in the memory of his suffering is to make an eschatological statement. Such a statement cannot be made more plausible through subsequent adaptation, nor is it capable of merely general verification. It remains controversial and controvertible; this power to scandalize belongs to its very meaning as something communicable. For the truth—remembered in the word "God"—of the passion of Jesus and of the history of human suffering is a truth whose recollection always painfully contradicts the expectations of the person recalling it.

The eschatological truth of the *memoria passionis* is not in fact deducible from our historical, social, and psychological systems. This is what first makes it a liberating truth at all. But this also prevents it by its very nature from ever fitting into our cognitive systems. Nor should this inability to fit in be removed by any "natural theology." Nevertheless, this natural theology does have its own justification. For if the eschatological truth of the *memoria passionis* is not to be expressed simply in empty tautologies and paradoxes, then it must be reflected within and determined by the concrete historical situation; the memory of the passion of Jesus must then be spelled out as a dangerously liberating memory within the supposed plausibilities of our society.

The Christian *memoria* insists that man's history of suffering does not belong simply to the prehistory of freedom, but rather that it is and remains within the history of freedom itself. The imaginative vision of future freedom nourishes itself from the remembrance of suffering; freedom degenerates wherever those who suffer are reduced more or less to a cliché and degraded to a faceless mass. And the Christian *memoria*, therefore, becomes a "provocative remembrance" which shocks one out of ever becoming prematurely reconciled to the so-called "facts" and "tendencies" of our technological society. It becomes a liberating memory over against the controls and mechanisms of the prevailing consciousness and its abstract ideal of emancipation. The Christian *memoria passionis* articulates itself as a memory which makes us free to suffer from the sufferings of others and to respect the prophetic witness unknown suffering embodies, despite the negative connotation given to suffering in our supposedly "progressive" society which makes it appear as something increasingly intolerable and even repugnant. The Christian *memoria* articulates itself as a memory which gives us the freedom to become old, although our public life appears today to reject old-age, experiencing it even as a "secret shame." The Christian *memoria* articulates itself as a memory which frees us for contemplation, although the hypnosis of work, performance, and planning seems to reach today into the farthest regions of our consciousness. It articulates itself as a memory which frees us to come to terms with our finitude and the conflicts of our contingency, although our society continuously suggests that life will become more advanced and "harmonious." Christian *memoria* articulates itself finally as a memory which frees us to respect the sufferings and hopes of the past and subject ourselves to the challenge of the dead.

A society which suppresses these dimensions in the history of freedom and in the understanding of freedom pays for this in the end with the increasing atrophy of that concrete freedom so necessary for the political imagination. It fails to develop any goals or priorities which could prevent the insidious accommodation of our freedom to the anonymous, impersonal framework of a computer society.

As a kind of initial thesis for this talk I put forward the proposal that the problem of the future is a primarily political and fundamentally social problem. We must now return to this position and ask: how is the Christian *memoria passionis* to be connected to political life at all and what would justify our doing this? What is it that connects the two? Would bringing them together not result in the destruction of both? As I have in fact emphasized, it is not a question here of introducing the Christian memory of suffering into the existing forms of political life; rather this *memoria passionis* has to become effective in transforming political life and structures, a transformation already shown to be the essential prerequisite for tackling the question of the future. Nonetheless, the fundamental question remains: doesn't political life fall victim to the reactionary influence of universalist norms once it is connected with the Christian *memoria passionis?* For this Christian *memoria passionis* as an eschatological *memoria* does in fact entail a particular interpretation of the meaning and subject of universal history!

But how can the question of the meaning and subject of the whole of history become relevant to political life? Doesn't every notion of a universal meaning of history in its political application lead to totalitarianism or at least to an uncritical, fanatical utopianism? All positivist theories of historical and political life insist on this danger. This positivist position cannot, however, itself avoid the question of whether its own rigorous rejection of the question of meaning doesn't in the end subject political life to a purely instrumental thinking and abandon it, in fact, in the long run to technocracy.

In contrast to this, classical Marxism and its theory of political life does of course decisively retain the question of the meaning and subject of universal history. Its intention here is essentially practical, to determine the content and goal of revolutionary praxis. For Marxism does indeed recognize a politically identifiable bearer of the meaning of history, namely the proletariat, which sets out to realize this meaning through its political praxis. But it is in fact difficult to understand how such a fusion of the meaning of history and political praxis doesn't end in a political totalitarianism which fails to reach the level of that transformation of political life which we seek for the sake of our future.

In its "liberal" theory of political life, classical Idealism also preserves the question of the meaning and subject of history. This position, however, differs from Marxism in recognizing no social and politically identifiable bearer of the totality of history; indeed, it rejects any attempt at political identification of this subject.

Hegel, for instance, calls the subject of the totality of history the *Weltgeist*, others speak of "nature," still others of "universal humanity." These are all apolitical predicates. Reference to the bearer and meaning of history remains here essentially abstract. Nevertheless, one sees that this abstract treatment of universal history can have an eminently practical and political meaning. It makes effectively possible the emancipation of political life from universal systems and universalist norms. Political life is set free to assume a purely pragmatic orientation; politics is determined solely by the "facts under discussion," the so-called *Sache selbst*, as one often hears. But are these "factual structures" really anything other than the very matter-of-fact structures and tendencies of our technological-economic processes? Where are we to find a contra-factual awareness providing a political alternative to these processes and their anonymous control if not in a pure decision-politics? Undoubtedly important in this liberal understanding of political life is its anti-totalitarian effect; nevertheless, as a positive statement it seems to provide no impulse for the political transformation we are seeking.

Let us examine once more the connection between the Christian *memoria passionis* and political life. In the remembrance of this suffering, God appears in his eschatological freedom as the subject and meaning of history as a whole. Now this implies, first of all, that for this *memoria* there is also no politically identifiable subject of universal history. Formulating it in all brevity, one can say that the meaning and goal of this universal history stand rather under God's so-called "eschatological proviso." The Christian *memoria* recalls the God of the passion of Jesus as the bearer of the universal history of suffering and, in the same movement, refuses any attempt to give political shape to this subject and establish it in power. Wherever a party, group, race, nation, or class—even the class of technocrats—tries to define and establish itself as this subject, the Christian *memoria* must rise up against this attempt and unmask it as political idolatry, as political ideology tending to totalitarianism or—in the language of the Apocalypse—pertaining to the "beast." In this way, the Christian *memoria passionis* serves also to liberate political life and protect it against totalitarianism. But now, as opposed to the liberal version of Idealism, this liberation is utopian in direction and not undefined. The Christian remembrance of suffering is, in fact, in its theological content an anticipatory memory; it contains the anticipation of a particular future of man, a future given to the suffering, the hopeless, the oppressed, the injured, the useless of this earth. That is why this memory of suffering does not in cold indifference surrender the political life orientated upon it to the game of social interests and powers. For its part, this game has, as its presupposition, conflict, so that it always favors the powerful, not the friendly, and always recognizes only that quantum of humanity which is the prerequisite for successfully putting across one's own interests. The memory of suffering, on the other hand, brings a new moral fantasy into political life, a new imaginative vision of the suffering of others which should ripen into an outflowing, uncalculating partiality for those without power and representation. And so the Christian memory of suffering could become, alongside other often subversive innovating powers in our society, the ferment for that new political life we are seeking on behalf of our human future.

Response to Johannes Metz

JOSEPH SITTLER

My comments will be related to the several sections of Professor Metz' paper.

The first section is called "The Socio-political Topos," and clearly says several true things. Principally this—that the Christian theological enterprise must be exercised within the context of social and political fact, the foci of its attention as well as data for reflection will be given by the changes and convulsions of that actuality—and that human suffering, perpetrated and steadily locked within economic, social, and political institutions is dangerously bitter and intolerable.

It is, indeed, out of such observations that the locating phrase "political theology" is fashioned. I am moved by this first section to two reflections: (1) theology in twentieth-century North America has not been unaware of this location of theological reflection, even if that awareness has been but wanly realized in Christian life and action. Less than 200 meters from this podium a faithful and enormously insightful theologian spelled that out with excruciating detail over more than three decades. (2) But even Reinhold Niebuhr did not denominate his incessant descriptive and analytical labor with such a title as to suppose the data he summoned to his work supplied him with a fundamental theology! His chair, Applied Christianity, was devoted to the exposition of neglected or forgotten implicates; it never sought to invade or capture the central stronghold of theological postulates. He thoroughly shook up those who operated there; but he was too deeply formed by the ductile nature of the historical to specify the formal method of theology with adjectives drawn from ever so urgent social and political forces.

The second section is called "Nature and History." My questions of this section are evoked by several characteristic sentences: " . . . political and social activity directed toward the future discovers its orientation, its 'norms', from a motivating context in history and not from a universal theory of nature" (pp. 122-123). Again: "There is no teleological, finalistic mediation between nature and man" (p. 123). Such statements, in my opinion, misstate the relation between God and man in nature and in history. For "nature" here means the given creation plus some theory of it. And the unpersuasive and presently developed status of theories of nature is not that about nature with which the ancient rubric of nature and Grace is presently involved; and to assume that it is is to oversimplify modern man's self-engagement with, and self-understanding within, the world of nature, and to dismiss the problem of man and his residency within the world-as-nature by dismissing nature as fact on the grounds of unwarranted theories about it. The eloquence and force of ecological fact is not identical with theories, teleological or other, about nature. That I *am* nature as well as history is fact, not only history, and therefore one must look carefully at the suggestions in this section that "historical consciousness" is alone the rubric for theology's reflections about the future.

There is for me always something strange and strained in theology's frequent efforts at total historization. God must have been about something before and during that complex operation, centration, complexification, and cerebralization which are the stages of my passage from sea water to this podium, and if my career as man should much longer humorlessly forget that and continue my bawdy historical performance as regards the creation, I may, under judgment, become an early leaver as I was, indeed, a late arriver in the creation.

Section three is called "The Future of Freedom in the Memory of Suffering." Before this powerful and eloquent section I can only stand in gratitude and admiration. And it is here, I think, where Professor Metz supplies us with the richest suggestions at a fundamental theological level. For what this section does is nothing less than to break a *theologia crucis* out of both privatized piety and cultic liturgical interment, and bring again together in *memoria passionis* the desolation of the primal suffering servant of God, the sufferings of the little peoples of the earth, and man's arrogant and fateful assault upon the creation which "groans in pain, waiting. . . ."

This paper, and particularly its last section, opens up afresh the ancient rubric of nature and grace. But it does that in a way that puts brakes upon its own momentum by ideologically dismissing the facticity of nature as both the placenta of man's reality and his creativity in the divine creation. This dismissal invites total focus upon historical freedom. A fateful achievement of such historical freedom in virtue of man's deepening knowledge of the structure and processes of the world-as-nature has been the subsumption of the world-as-nature under the olympian decisional realm of man-as-history.

Nature is patient and apparently compliant within this process. But nature has her own created integrity; she is patient but implacable. And when the double gratuity of grace as in the divine redemption and in the divine creation is totally historicized—the theological task is bent—by anthropological presumption. It will tend to be wrong about man's fulfillment because it will be wrong about man and nature. These comments, I think, are fundamental. They are not correctable within the idea of nature which controls the paper. But such a correction would not weaken or "inhibit" the superb elaboration of *ex memoria passionis* as a primary theme for fundamental theology but rather release, expand, and enforce it.

Response to Johannes Metz

LEWIS S. FORD

We have come here to reflect together on the theme of hope and man's future, but other themes insistently clamor for attention. Professor Moltmann suggested that our chosen theme would have been most welcome five years ago, but now the hopes of the 1960's are gone, and our *Lebensgefühl* is much rather one of frustration—the feeling of having been betrayed. "Hope and the Future of Man" sounds too optimistic, too deceptive, too good to be true. Now Professor Metz, in his effort to respond sensitively to our present situation, feels obliged to stress the reality of suffering, particularly the memory of suffering which keeps us protesting our freedom against the social systems of our technological civilization. Why is this so? Why do frustration and suffering so crowd in upon our concern for hope?

No doubt many political or sociological reasons might be given. The hopes of the war on poverty have floundered as the war drags on—and on. The hope of a revolutionary renewal of academic life —not only here but I suspect more particularly in Germany—has become mired down in bureaucratic procedure, when all that seems to be accomplished is an Americanization of faculty governance: the endless committee meetings. Those hopes so profoundly generated by Pope John's call for a renewal of the Church have encountered hardships and fallen upon evil days. The list could be almost endlessly extended. Rather than consider these, however, I want to focus our attention upon a different sort of reason—a philosophical one rooted in the nature of hope in a final consummation.

Suppose we assume with Teilhard that the evolutionary process points to increasing convergence and complexification, or with Pannenberg that the essence of history can only be realized in its end. On what grounds can we affirm that this final convergence yields the full personalization of man rather than his collectivization or destruction, or that the end of history is a general resurrection instead of the final judgment—the second death? Does God guarantee a final victory? Can we have the confidence that God will finally bring about the triumph of good, no matter how badly we mess it up? If so, its coming is inevitable; why need we strive so hard to bring it about? If so, the risks of this world lose their seriousness, for there is no ultimate risk. If the good triumphs no matter what, the sufferings God allows us to endure on the way lose their meaning because he could have accomplished his purposes without them.

But what if, on the other hand, there is no final triumph of good, and we simply face the bleak future of more of the same? Professor Mooney eloquently pointed out this other side to the problem. It is all too easy to dismiss Teilhard as a facile optimist, without penetrating to the root of his desperate vision, for Teilhard was deeply sensitive to the growing hopelessness of modern man. Without the assurance of tomorrow, can we go on living? Hope releases the energies of man, and the lure of a better future is the only reason for any striving. Proximate hopes, however, must be situated within an horizon of ultimate hope. For all the hopes and strivings of man become revealed as utter vanity if the final end of the universe is simply a wasting away into nothingness.

The logic of the situation seems inexorable: without hope, we are lost and still in our sins. This hope requires an ultimate horizon which must be both real and good, otherwise our hope is based on an illusion. But an inevitable triumph of good undercuts the seriousness and risk of the human task, and gives the lie to its manifold sufferings.

We are left with this dilemma so long as we look for the meaning of the world along the temporal axis of its future. If the value and purpose of all our suffering and striving is finally vested in its temporal outcome, we cease to have any genuine basis for hope unless the goodness of that end is assured. Process theism, however, radically shifts the locus for our hope: the ultimate meaning of the world is not to be found in its future, but in its on-going contribution to the life of God. The ultimate horizon of hope is situated not at the end of history but in the present experience of God. All of our deeds and actions finally come to nought in this temporal scene, but not before they have become a permanent enrichment of the divine life.

There are strong metaphysical reasons why Whiteheadians resist any notion of an ultimate end of history or a final consummation of the evolutionary process. If all being lies in becoming, the end of becoming would signify the annihilation of all things, including God, for the continuation of the divine concrescence requires a constant enrichment of novelty from the world. The creative rhythm of the one and the many fortunately prevents that by insuring that the world process will necessarily continue forever. Furthermore, God's appetition for the actualization of all pure possibilities requires an infinity of cosmic epochs for the world. I envision an endless series of expansions and contractions of the universe, in which all the outcomes and achievements of each cosmic epoch are crushed to bits in a final cataclysmic contraction, to provide a mass/

energy capable of assuming a novel physical organization in the next expansion. The inner electron shell of all atoms in our present observable universe, for example, contains no more than two electrons. But in another cosmic epoch these inner shells might contain three electrons, thereby generating a radically different chemistry of molecular combinations, to say nothing of biology and culture. Only in some such fashion will it be possible for God to pursue his aim at the actualization of all pure possibilities, each in its due season.

For our present purposes, however, it is more important to recognize that there are no religious reasons for insisting on an end to the process *if* the meaning of the world and the ground of our hope is to be found in the enrichment of divine experience. There can be all sorts of penultimate consummations in the future, but none need be the bearers of such ultimate significance which demands that it must necessarily be unambiguously good.

We have hope in God, but it is equally true that God has hope in all of his creatures, trusting us to accomplish his purposes by actualizing the lures he provides. God is infinitely rich in possibility, but deficient in actuality, for all that is actual is finite, limited, and ultimately arbitrary in character. The world is rich in actuality, but deficient in possibility. Each provides the novel enrichment of the other in an ecological balance. God's hopes for us may never be fulfilled, and that is the risk he takes upon himself, suffering the pain and sorrows of the world which are the outcome of our failures; nevertheless, he can take the least promising result of our doings and clothe it with meaning out of the inexhaustible resources of his conceptual possibilities.[1]

Now Professor Metz catches us up short by insisting upon suffering: ". . . it is suffering that opposes an affirmative theory of reconciliation between man and nature . . . . the anthropocentric of suffering . . . prevails over against every cosmocentrism" (p. 123-124) and requires us to interpret nature from the viewpoint of history. Here are two distinct issues: nature and history and the anthropocentricity of suffering.

If by nature we mean phenomena investigated and understood in terms of causal regularities expressible in scientific laws, we agree: nature must be understood in terms of history, not vice versa, for history combines objective regularity with novelty, contingency, and freedom.[2] Process is misunderstood if it is thought to be merely the process of nature. Process also provides the abstract structure for the novelty, contingency, and freedom which finds its concrete embodiment in history. Philosophy, however, is methodologically restricted to the description of the abstract process, for we must look to the facts—to what has actually taken place—for the contingent, concrete embodiment. A process natural theology can outline the contours of God's activity, but this can never substitute for the revelation of God in history, since it is only by reflection upon the historical witness to God's dealings with his people that we can discern anything of his concrete fullness.

But we must reject Professor Metz's anthropocentricity of suffering. Paul testifies "that the whole creation has been groaning in travail together until now." (Rom. 8:22) Suffering is universal, inherent in the very character of teleology. But care must be taken here lest we think of teleology in Aristotelian terms. By teleology I intend the causal effectiveness of the lure of novel possibilities for actualization. If the world were completely determined by antecedent causation, there could be no genuine novelty, neither evolutionary emergence nor historical freedom. If events are not fully determined by their causal past, then the lure of future possibility must provide the additional causal factor. But possibility is inherently indeterminate. We never confront just one or two alternatives, though for simplicity's sake we often like to think so; we confront a whole range of alternatives, each imperceptibly sliding over into the next in a continuous fashion. Possibility, in itself, lacks individuality and hence causal effectiveness by itself. A possibility only becomes individual and distinct through decision, which is the paring down and elimination of all other alternatives to leave just that single one which is actualized. In this sense, teleology is only possible in terms of decision. God coordinates the activities of the world by providing each creature with a value-ordering of the possibilities confronting it, but it is the creature who decides—for better or worse, for only that which is finite can bring about what is finite and actual. Such a plurality of separate decisions necessarily entails the risk of conflict and loss and this is what we experience as suffering and triviality.

Thus far I have been mostly clearing the ground by explaining the ultimate basis for hope despite the suffering we endure with our fellow creatures. I want to address myself to one positive task. Professor Metz has spoken eloquently and insightfully about the power of dangerous memories. The memory of suffering liberates us from the narrowness of institutional and instrumental values by forcing us to become aware of other values and ideals these exclude. The most serious conflicts are not between good and evil, but between good and good, where in the name of its cherished ideal, whether that be "the free world" or "law and order," a country crushes the aspirations and ideals of others, whether they be there in Vietnam or here in the ghettoes. The whole busing issue reveals the conflict of a whole cluster of ideals: integration, racial balance, neighborhood schools, the right to ethnic solidarity. Only through suffering will the full range of relevant ideals be felt. Professor Metz also pointed to that supreme memory of suffering we confess to: the crucifixion of the man who bears the hope of the world—crucified in the name of the cherished ideals of those entrusted with the promises of God to his people Israel. But I do not understand how resurrection follows upon crucifixion in providing the hope of mankind from Professor Metz's perspective, and would like to sketch briefly my own perspective on the resurrection.

I borrow here from Professor Cobb's speculations on the possible interpenetration of persons. The individual person in this full interpenetration, Cobb writes, " is no longer concerned with a personal future, for the whole future is its future, as the whole past is its past. Each lives from all and for all. In such a future all that matters about our selfhood is preserved, but it is continued, developed, transformed, and purified, passing from the compartmentalized and protected psyche that we now know into myriads of free and open selves unconcerned with their peculiar lines of inheritance" (p. 14). Cobb is writing here of disembodied psyches surviving the death of their bodies. Whiteheadians are by no means of one mind about life after death, and while I appreciate its theoretical possibility, I existentially reject its actuality. I would rather apply these words to the life of the early Church. The memory of Jesus' life and death so broke open the lives of his disciples that they could live from all and for all. They became joined together in that body which is the body of Christ's resurrection. Christ is the word of God as addressed to man in his particular condition, but the Word addresses every species of creatures, calling it to creative fulfillment beyond itself in the evolutionary advance of the world. Man is no exception, and here I gladly avail myself of Teilhard's notions of convergence and complexification, seeing in the body of Christ a new biological evolutionary emergence, taking us beyond the limitations of individual human beings. Jesus is the incarnation of this divine address to mankind, but as John Knox points out, this incarnation takes place through the total Christ-event, including the life, death, and resurrection.[3] Jesus died so that Christ might be born. God addresses the members of this body through Christ as the memory of Jesus which focuses for us the desires and aims of God as related to the interpenetration of our concerns with one another in love. In Christ we have become a new creation; old things have passed away.

If I am asked to bear witness to this reality of Christ today, I must confess I see only fragmentary and ambiguous realizations. If the Church invisible is the body of Christ, then its institutions are Christ's bones—necessary and essential for the upbuilding of the whole body, but useless apart from life and flesh. I do not know whether we confront a living reality or the skeletal remains, but if God raised up Christ once, he can do it again. This to me is the second coming: Christ will come again and again to be incarnate in human communities until this evolutionary emergence can sustain itself and thrive, provided we have not destroyed ourselves in the meantime.

Finally, however, I must emphasize that this hope for man in the future of Christ always remains a penultimate hope. It need not bear the heavy weight of inevitability lest we lose all basis for serious striving. Our ultimate hope lies not in the future of Christ, but in the life of God.

NOTES

[1] I have developed and defended these claims in greater detail in "Divine Persuasion and the Triumph of Good," *Process Philosophy and Christian Thought,* edited by Delwin Brown, Ralph E. James, Jr., and Gene Reeves (Indianapolis: Bobbs-Merrill, 1971), pp. 287-304.

[2] Thus on Professor Metz's view there can be a genuine history of nature. I do not see that he simply dismisses nature as Professor Sittler suggests.

[3] See *The Humanity and Divinity of Christ* (Cambridge University Press, 1967) and *The Church and the Reality of Christ* (New York: Harper & Row, 1962).

Hope and the Future of Man:

A Reflection

DANIEL DAY WILLIAMS

Each person brought to the conference on hope his conception of the meaning of the gospel message, and his own perspective on hope. Each left the conference with some questions sharpened, some new perspectives, and probably with a conviction about where the theologies of promise and fulfillment for mankind must do further work. What I can do here is to give some reflections of one participant about what we were hearing from one another, and where we seemed to be moving.

We knew from the outset that Teilhardians, theologians of hope in the recent style of Continental theology, and process theologians have a common concern to bring to the world with its aspirations, its agonies, and its despair the gospel of hope based upon what God has done and will do in Jesus Christ. All three schools see the meaning of the Christian faith as eschatologically determined. Life is understood through what we shall be.

We discovered that we approach this search for a doctrine of hope in rather different ways. While the word "approach" is vague, we really need to speak of three approaches to the expression of Christian hope. We were already aware of some differences in theological method, and on the whole they were represented as might have been expected, but there were some surprises. The theology of hope as developed by the Continental theologians and represented also by Carl Braaten may be described as confessional in method. The theologians work from within the biblical message as they interpret it, and move out to conclusions about the meaning of the eschatological structure of faith. However, Pannenberg incorporates a metaphysical element derived from a philosophical interpretation of the unity of history, and he comes even closer than one might have expected to the method of the process theologians. Moltmann's book, *Theology of Hope,* is developed in a biblical confessional exegetical style; but his paper in the conference argues for the theologians' entering into an analysis of immediate human problems and letting that analysis reflect back on the ethical convictions underlying the Christian life.

Process theologians are frankly concerned with a metaphysical structure as one indispensable context for interpreting the word of God in Jesus Christ. They develop a metaphysical view of God, time and history and appeal for its validity to concrete experience informed by the light of the gospel. This does not prevent them from speculative ventures concerning the future and the meaning of life beyond death, as John Cobb's paper shows. Process theologians take the issue of hope to refer both to present expectations and to future possibilities within the divine redemptive action.

The Teilhardian perspective, like that of process theology, draws upon a general scheme of understanding the world as described by science and interpreted in a cosmic development toward final unity. In Philip Hefner's paper and in the discussion generally the Teilhardians put less emphasis upon the details of the cosmological scheme and more upon the spiritual vision which makes it possible for persons here and now to live religiously by participating in the slow, painful growth of humanity toward unity. To this participant this mystical and moral passion for sharing the creative action which is God's work in the world was the most impressive feature of the Teilhardian optimism, not the affirmation of a final success at Omega point, but the hopefulness about a significant ethical and religious life in the present age.

Of the many issues opened up by these approaches I mention three.

First, there is the question of how to relate the eschatological structure of hope with its vision of the "last things" to present problems of social and political history. Death is conquered by resurrection. But what does this mean for millions dying of starvation, or the millions of people dying at the hands of other men? All the contributions to the conference had this reality of the human condition explicitly in view. Every theological point of view was stated with awareness of the need for relating ultimate hope to immediate human problems. But I believe it is fair to say that the connection was not clearly made. What is different about the way one meets the present fulfillments and frustrations of life in the light of eschatology and what is different about a Christian theory of social causes because of the eschatological outlook?

There is for example the issue of utopianism, sharply raised by Carl Braaten at the beginning of the conference and penetratingly dealt with by Johannes Metz at the end. We are forced to ask: What kind of concrete involvement in present causes, actions, and commitments can we reasonably, faithfully, and fruitfully assert when we live by the ultimate promise of the kingdom? Johannes Metz' moving plea for a politics rooted in the memory of suffering aims to set us free from utopianism; but how do we then move to guidance about what causes are worth pursuing in the present history of suffering? Jürgen Moltmann's insightful analysis of biomedical problems leaves him open to the question Ogden asks about the bearing of this mode of analysis on the eschatological faith rooted in the cross and the resurrection of Jesus Christ.

The planners of this conference had in mind a succeeding conference in which the bearing of the Christian faith on such specific and critical issues could be explored by theologians with people from other disciplines. The present conference certainly led up to and pointed to the need for such a further exploration.

The second question concerns the truth of what we say and how we say it when we speak of hope and particularly of the final hope for victory over sin and death. The credibility gap between traditional theology and contemporary modes of thought informed by science, philosophy, and political outlooks is very great. That gap is likely to appear even larger when we speak of the future for then we speak of that realm where we have no present experience, and where we live by the promise, not the immediate reality. Here is need for further clarification of the relation between biblical exegesis and philosophic structure; between the standpoint of faith and a critical reflection on experience. Metz says there is "no mediation between nature and man." Teilhardians and process theologians hold that man is unintelligible except as participant in an evolving nature which sustains him. The relation between Moltmann's confessional standpoint in *Theology of Hope* and his exploration of the present issues involved in new medical techniques raises important methodological questions. Does the Christian have special insight into these issues and if so where is its source and how is it related to the insight which comes from secular work with such problems?

Finally there appears to run through the discussions an issue about the form and substance of Christian eschatology. It is the question whether Christian hope must be expressed in the affirmation of one final event which constitutes the absolute reversal of all the unresolved problems of human existence, or whether the Christian hope can be expressed in the form of a confidence in God in the midst of a creative adventure which need have no end, but which is open for the creative work of God forever. The theological perspectives here represented except that of the process theologians appear to move in the first pattern. For the former views the eschaton is the contradiction or complete reversal of the risk, suffering, and uncertainty of the present. The process theologians, on the other hand, regard creativity and the freedom to participate in it as one aspect of the perfection of love.

The issue is not whether there is hope for a meaningful life and participation in God's life after death. John Cobb shows that this is within the outlook of process thought. The issue is the subtle one of whether meaningful life here and now requires hope in an absolute end point such as the Omega point of the Teilhardians, or the final event of which Pannenberg speaks. The process view seems to sacrifice absolute victory for absolute openness to creativity. Is such an eschatology biblical and meaningful?

In all three views there is the conviction that everything in nature and history is subject to the redemptive work of God. There is a consensus that God is at work in time, bearing with his world, and going before it, making present life intelligible, and filling with hope our present work, suffering, and dying through the future which he holds before us. Christians understand that hope as it is given in the story of God's covenant with Israel and its climax in the life, death, and resurrection of Jesus. The hope there released into the world is for the whole creation and every creature.

The issues dealt with in the conference require the concentrated and critical attention not only of theologians but of every person who is seeking faith for the times in which we now live. The coming together of people of these different outlooks and their holding such conversation was itself a contribution to the spirit of hopefulness among us. Theological work can be done today not out of an assumption that any one school possesses all truth, but out of the hope born of the gospel message that the Spirit which binds us together will guide us into the Truth.

Biographical Notes

EWERT H. COUSINS is Associate Professor of Theology at Fordham University and President of the American Teilhard de Chardin Association. He is the editor of the anthology *Process Theology.*

JOHN B. COBB, JR., is Ingraham Professor of Theology at the School of Theology at Claremont, California. He is the author of *A Christian Natural Theology: Based on the Thought of Alfred North Whitehead* and co-editor of the journal, *Process Studies.*

PHILIP HEFNER is Professor of Systematic Theology at the Lutheran School of Theology at Chicago. He is the author of *Faith and the Vitalities of History* and *The Promise of Teilhard.*

CARL E. BRAATEN is Professor of Theology at the Lutheran School of Theology at Chicago. He is the author of *The Future of God* and *Christ and Counter-Christ.*

WOLFHART PANNENBERG is Professor at the University of Munich, Germany. He is the author of *Jesus: God and Man* and the two-volume work, *Basic Questions in Theology.*

JURGEN MOLTMANN is Professor at the University of Tübingen in Germany. He is the author of *Theology of Hope* and *Religion, Revolution, and the Future.*

JOHANNES B. METZ is Dean of the Catholic Faculty and Professor of Theology in the University of Münster, Germany. Among his works in English is *Theology of the World.*

DONALD P. GRAY is Associate Professor in the Department of Religious Studies at Manhattan College, New York. He is the author of *The One and the Many: Teilhard de Chardin's Vision of Unity.*

DANIEL DAY WILLIAMS is Roosevelt Professor of Systematic Theology at the Union Theological Seminary in New York City. He is the author of *The Spirit and the Forms of Love* and *God's Grace and Man's Hope.*

CHRISTOPHER F. MOONEY, S.J. is President and Professor of Theology at Woodstock College, New York City. He is the author of *Teilhard de Chardin and the Mystery of Christ* and *The Making of Man*.

SCHUBERT M. OGDEN is Professor of Theology at the Perkins School of Theology, Southern Methodist University, Dallas, Texas. He is the author of *The Reality of God and Other Essays* and *Christ Without Myth*.

JOSEPH SITTLER is Professor of Theology at the Divinity School of the University of Chicago. He is the author of *Essays on Nature and Grace*.

LEWIS S. FORD is Associate Professor of Philosophy at the Pennsylvania State University, University Park, Pennsylvania, and co-editor of the journal, *Process Studies*.